is for Baldwin

An Alphabet Tour of the Baldwin Library of Historical Children's Literature

Edited by Suzan Alteri

An Alphabet Tour of the Baldwin Library of Historical Children's Literature

LIBRARY PRESS@UF
AN IMPRINT OF UF PRESS AND GEORGE A. SMATHERS LIBRARIES
UNIVERSITY of FLORIDA

535 Library West
PO Box 117000
Gainesville, FL 32611-7000
https://go.ufl.edu/librarypress
librarypress@uflib.ufl.edu

Edited by Suzan Alteri
Published by LibraryPress@UF
Designed by Tracy E. MacKay-Ratliff

Identifiers: ISBN 978-1-944455-11-8 (paperback)
Cataloging-in-Publication Data
Names: Alteri, Suzan, editor. | George A. Smathers Libraries, publisher.
Title: B is for Baldwin: An alphabet tour of the Baldwin Library / edited by Suzan Alteri.
Description: Gainesville, FL : Library Press @ UF, 2022 | Summary: The Baldwin Library of Historical Children's Literature, part of the Special and Area Studies collection in Smathers Library at the University of Florida holds over 120,000 volumes published in Great Britain and the United States from the mid-1600s to the current moment. In addition to containing many rare and colorful books, it serves as an important research collection for scholars of children's literature, childhood studies, and more. B is for Baldwin presents a tour of the collection via the letters of the alphabet.
Subjects: LCSH: Baldwin Library. | Children's literature—Study and teaching (Higher). | Libraries—Special collections—Children's literature.
Classification: LCC Z1038.B28 B24 2022
OCLC no. 1322443099
Alma IZ MMS ID 99383348865206597
Link to Primo record—https://ufl-flvc.primo.exlibrisgroup.com/permalink/01FALSC_UFL/1e2g8es/alma99383348865206597
Printed in the United States of America.
FIRST EDITION.

is for Baldwin

An Alphabet Tour of the Baldwin Library of Historical Children's Literature

Edited by Suzan Alteri

B is for Baldwin

An Alphabet Tour of the Baldwin Library of Historical Children's Literature

Contents

▲ ***Mother Goose the Old Nursery Rhymes,*** Illustrated by Arthur Rackham, published by William Heinemann (1913).

14. In happy Eden see them plac'd,
Who stood or fell for all our race:
In a sweet bower, compos'd for love,
This happy pair might safely rove.
There was no curse upon that ground,
Nor changing grief there to be found;
There nothing could their joys control,
Nor mar the pleasures of the soul.
5. A Griffin here you may behold,
Half beast half fowl is he;
Once more do but the leaf downfold,
A stranger sight you'll see
16. Had they obey'd their Maker's voice,
And made eternal bliss their choice,
Then everlasting life had been
The lot of all the sons of men.
But Satan came now in disguise,
To blind this happy couple's eyes:
Saying, this fruit now eat, and you
Like God shall good and evil know.
12. O Man! now see, thou art but dust;
Thy gold and silver is but rust;
Thy time is come, thy glass is spent;
What is there that can Death prevent?
1. Adam comes first upon the stage,
And Eve from out his side,
Who was given him in marriage;
Turn up and see his bride.
7. Now I've escap'd the Eagle's Claws
And am from danger free,
I'll set my heart to gather Gold;
Turn down the Leaf and see.
3 Eyes look not on the mermaid's face,
And ears hear not her song;
Her features have an alluring grace,
More charming than her tongue.
17. Eve did the fatal Apple take
And gave her husband, who did eat;
Thus Adam fell to his disgrace,
From his native righteousness.
Now every thought that roves abroad,
Is known to a sin-hating God:
His perfect law he will maintain,
Ah! He'll reward the fall of man.
8. A Heart here is, oppress'd with care,
What salve can cure the same?
Under the leaf you'll find a cure:
Lift up and see how plain.
19. Or who before his awful bar
In his own righteousness appear?
The sons of Adam, since the fall,
To death are subject, one and all.
But to the Serpent it is said,
The Woman's seed shall bruise thy head;
Though Adam harken'd to his bride,
Who pluck'd the fruit which was deny'd.

▲ ***Metamorphosis, or, A Transformation of Pictures: with Poetical Explanations: for The Amusement of Young Persons***, by Benjamin Sands, printed by Solomon Wiatt (1807).

B is for Baldwin

Introduction

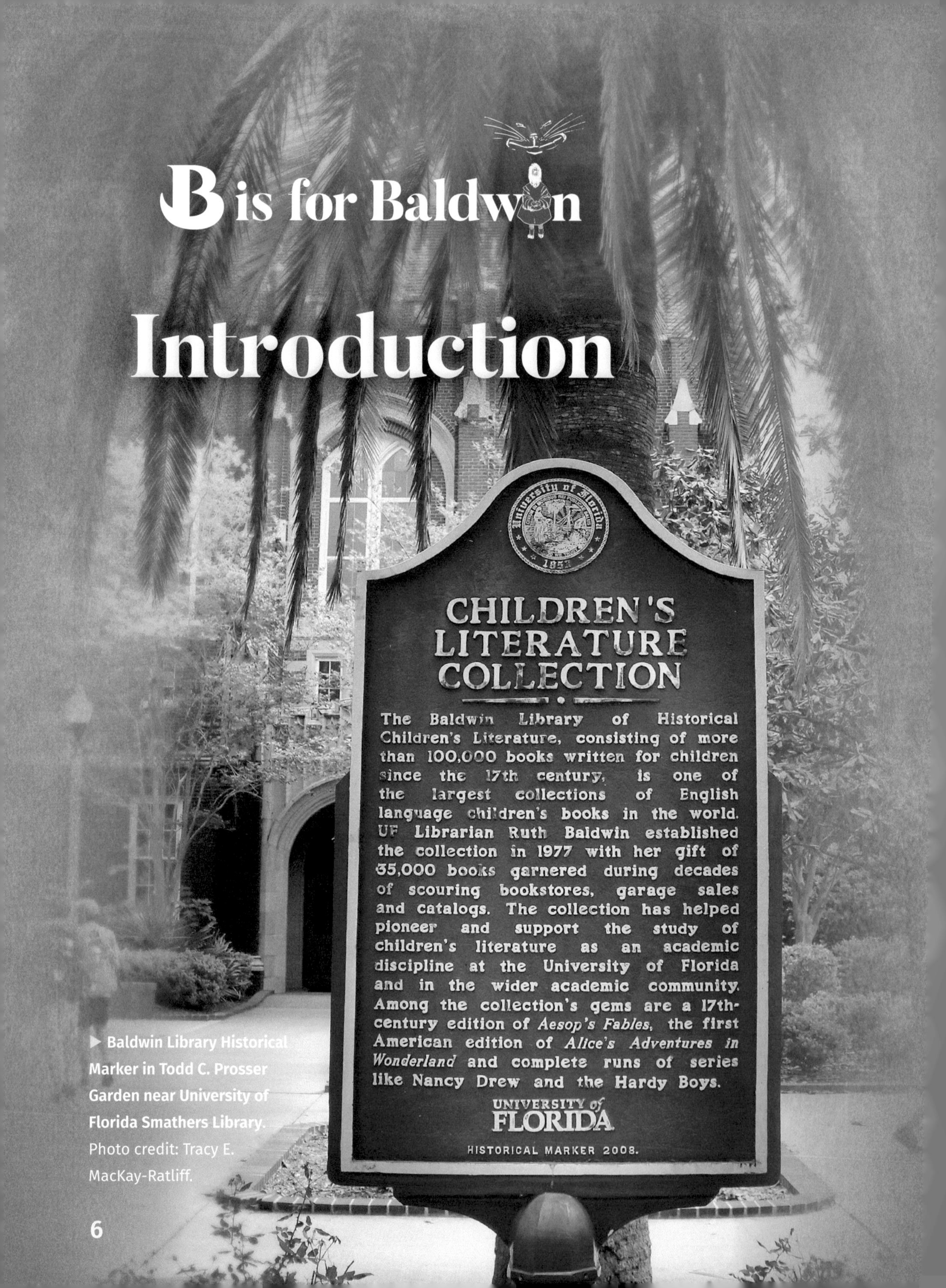

CHILDREN'S LITERATURE COLLECTION

The Baldwin Library of Historical Children's Literature, consisting of more than 100,000 books written for children since the 17th century, is one of the largest collections of English language children's books in the world. UF Librarian Ruth Baldwin established the collection in 1977 with her gift of 35,000 books garnered during decades of scouring bookstores, garage sales and catalogs. The collection has helped pioneer and support the study of children's literature as an academic discipline at the University of Florida and in the wider academic community. Among the collection's gems are a 17th-century edition of *Aesop's Fables*, the first American edition of *Alice's Adventures in Wonderland* and complete runs of series like Nancy Drew and the Hardy Boys.

UNIVERSITY of FLORIDA

HISTORICAL MARKER 2008.

▶ **Baldwin Library Historical Marker in Todd C. Prosser Garden near University of Florida Smathers Library.** Photo credit: Tracy E. MacKay-Ratliff.

The Baldwin Editorial Collective:
Suzan Alteri, Poushali Bhadury, Kenneth Kidd, Laurie N. Taylor

The Baldwin Library of Historical Children's Literature, part of Special and Area Studies Collections at the University of Florida (UF), is one of the largest and most comprehensive collections of children's books in the world.

The legacy of Dr. Ruth Baldwin, the Baldwin Library holds over 120,000 volumes published in Great Britain and the United States from the mid-1600s to the current moment. A library science professor at Louisiana State University—and a lively, sometimes intimidating person—Baldwin began collecting children's books on weekends and during vacations, drawing on her modest academic salary and typically paying no more than 5 cents for a book. By 1977, she had amassed a private collection of around 35,000 volumes, ranging from chapbooks to series books to nineteenth-century periodicals and early movables. At that point Baldwin thought of her collection as a research library, and began searching for an institutional site for it since her home institution wasn't interested. She had conversations with the University of Illinois, the University of Texas, the University of Denver, Stanford University, and even the Library of Congress. A delegation from UF's English Department visited and persuaded her that the University of Florida was the best place, and Baldwin agreed, with the condition that she come along as Curator. Baldwin retired from the Curator role in 1988 and was succeeded by Rita J.

▲ ***The History of Little Fanny: Exemplified in a Series of Figures,*** printed by S. and J. Fuller (1810).

Smith, who wrote the lovely entry on Baldwin in this book. Rita and the subsequent Curator, Suzan Alteri, further expanded the collection to include 20th century books, as well as periodicals and technological/optical toys and games that can be "read" like texts. Smith, in particular, worked to get the entire collection cataloged to make it accessible to patrons who were not always able to visit. Thanks to their efforts, and those of the newest Curator, Dr. Ramona Caponegro, the physical collection continues to grow, while the Baldwin Library Digital Collection is the largest open access full-text children's literature collections in the world, with over 6,000 individual titles. This digital collection was created from a series of National Endowment for the Humanities grants (see "N is for NEH").

In 2008, the Baldwin Library was recognized by the UF Alumni Association as "an historical campus site" and given its own marker in a special dedication ceremony. Through such designations, the Alumni Association seeks "to highlight and publicize the research that is accomplished on campus and draw attention to the rich resources that are available to both students and alumni." The Baldwin Library is indeed a rich resource for significant discoveries about children's literary and material culture. We can learn a lot about literature and culture—about history in all its complexities—by looking at the books therein.

Much of the value of the collection stems from Baldwin's collecting philosophy. She was interested in materials that children handled, collecting less-than-pristine editions of just about any printed text. Researchers can thus study popular materials that have not otherwise been preserved, at least not comprehensively. Over the years the curators have found a remarkable array of objects inside the books, from locks of hair to letters to baseball cards. Many of the books in the collection also have wonderful inscriptions or other sorts of paratext (texts within the main text). Some children's books were literally made from other books or paper materials, and you can see evidence of that repurposing. A talented undergraduate student, Kristina C. Wilson, wrote a fascinating essay about this and even curated a fabulous exhibition on the Baldwin Library's "somnotexts," meaning fragments of other texts that "sleep" in the spines or bindings of children's books and are revealed through use or abuse. The materials in the Baldwin Library, in other words, are fascinating as material objects as well as narratives. Baldwin also collected multiple editions of the same text—the collection holds some 300 editions of Daniel Defoe's *Robinson Crusoe*, for example—making possible comparisons among editions. Baldwin also was notorious for acquiring everything, at least everything published in English, and the size and scope of the Baldwin Library makes it very valuable as a research repository. It affords opportunities not only for examining individual texts but also for studying a large and evolving corpus of children's literature across time.

▲ ***Robinson Crusoe,*** **by Daniel Defoe, illustrated by Willy Pogány, published by George G. Harrap & Co. (1914).**

The Library has enabled much exciting scholarship over the years, undertaken by UF faculty, graduate students, and researchers across the world. In her entry "B is for (Ruth) Baldwin," Rita Smith mentions that Gillian Avery drew heavily on Baldwin holdings in her groundbreaking study *Behold the Child: American Children and Their Books, 1621-1922.* UF PhD alum and *B is for Baldwin* contributor Megan A. Norcia researched woman-authored geography primers and Robinsonades from the Baldwin for her book, *X Marks the Spot: British Women Map the Empire, 1790-1895*; Norcia also looked at Baldwin holdings for her second book *Gaming Empire in Children's British Board Games, 1836-1860.* Another *B is for Baldwin* contributor and PhD alum, Julie Sinn Cassidy, worked extensively with the Baldwin's collection of Little Golden books in her dissertation. Other academic books indebted to Baldwin holdings include Kara K. Keeling and Scott T. Pollard's *Table Lands: Food in Children's Literature*; Lissa Paul's *Eliza Fenwick: Early Modern Feminist*; Lucy Rollin's critical edition of Twain's *The Adventures of Tom Sawyer*; Eugene Giddens and Zoe Jaques' *Lewis Carroll's* Alice's Adventures in Wonderland *and* Through the Looking-Glass: *A Publishing History*; and Giddens' *Christmas Books for Children.* Numerous other scholars have drawn on Baldwin holdings, among them Lawrence Darton, Richard Wunderlich, Lynne Vallone, Susan Miller, Donelle Rue, Sue Chen, Alan Rauch, Claudia Nelson, Courtney Weikle-Mills, Joe Sutliff Sanders, and JoAnn Conrad. UF graduate students who have gone on to publish Baldwin-based research include Cari Keebaugh, Horacio Sierra, Emily Murphy, Ramona Caponegro, Lisa Dusenberry, Cathlena Martin, Rebekah Fitzsimmons, and Emily Faith Brooks.

UF English offers a PhD track in children's literature and is also home to the Center for Children's Literature and Culture, directed by Dr. John Cech. The Baldwin affords UF children's literature scholars the chance to conduct research at home, as it were; at the same time, UF English recognized the value of the collection in the first place and helped spirit it to Florida.

While the Baldwin Library is a book collection, it does hold some papers, including materials related to the life and career of Louise Seaman Bechtel, the first (female) editor of a children's or juvenile division within a major publishing house. The Bechtel papers came to the Baldwin from the Cerimon Foundation, created by Bechtel specifically to endow the Baldwin Library in support of visiting researchers. The Association for Library Service to Children (ALSC), a group within the American Library Association, administers the Louise Seaman Bechtel Fellowship, which provides a grant to children's librarians to spend up to a month studying in the Baldwin Library on a project of their devising and then report on their findings. Over the years many Bechtel Fellows have conducted all manner of research projects, and some have published their work. Articles by Bechtel Fellows have appeared in *Children and Libraries* across the years, among them Jane Marino's "Joyful Noise: A Study of Children's Music at the Baldwin Library of Historical Children's Literature"; Jacqueline Spratlin Rogers's "Picturing the Child in Nineteenth-Century Literature: The Artist, the Child, and a Changing Society"; and Charmette Kendrick's "The Goblins Will Get You! Horror in Children's Literature from the Nineteenth Century." Bechtel Fellows contribute to the collective knowledge and make wonderful ambassadors for the Baldwin Library.

The Baldwin is a teaching collection, too, used with undergraduate and graduate classes in a variety of disciplines, English especially. Suzan Alteri collaborated on a class with UF English professor Terry Harpold; Alteri writes about that experience in her article "The Classroom as Salon: A Collaborative Project on Daniel Defoe's *Robinson Crusoe*." UF English professor Kenneth Kidd has thrice taught a Baldwin-based graduate seminar, collaborating with Rita and then with Suzan; his article "The Child, the Scholar, and the Children's Literature Archive" is part reflection on that experience. Former UF English PhD student Kristen Gregory co-taught (with Alteri) an undergraduate special topics course on death in children's literature, which culminated in some beautiful collaborative digital exhibits. More recently, Dr. Rae Yan designed an inventive Baldwin assignment for her section of The Golden Age of Children's Literature, an upper-level undergraduate course; Yan asked her students to compose a scholarly introduction for a work that sparked their interest from the collection. Four of those fantastic introductions —by Hugh Hickman, Chloe Kuka, Sofia Padrón, and Tiffany Teska—appeared in a special issue of *SOURCE: The Magazine of the University of Florida George A. Smathers Libraries.* Other undergraduate students have pursued theses

▲ ***Alice's Adventures in Wonderland,*** by Lewis C. Carroll, illustrated by John Tenniel, published by Henry Altemus Company (c.1897).

or other long research projects drawing on Baldwin resources.

Not everything about historical children's literature is admirable, and some Baldwin-based research has rightly grappled with the racism, misogyny, and xenophobia of some children's materials. There are some bad books in the stacks. In 2018, Alteri and two library colleagues, Stephanie Birch and Hélène Huet, curated a Baldwin-based exhibit entitled "Racism, Representation, and Resistance in Children's Literature 1800-2015," which gave dual focus to racist materials and to anti-racist materials by African American authors in particular. The materials featured included American, British, and European titles, some of which were available digitally also. The physical exhibit ran from August 13 to October 5, 2018, and an online version is still hosted on UF's Smathers exhibits website. Alteri also worked with Noah Mullens, now in the English doctoral program, on an online exhibit dealing with diversity-critical events in US history and their representation in as well as impact on children's literature. A related initiative was a multi-year project dedicated to diversifying digital children's literature collections, a collaboration between a UF team and researchers based largely in the UK, funded by the UK's Arts and Humanities Research Council. Such projects reflect UF's commitment to acknowledging social ills and promoting diversity, equity, and inclusion. We have a responsibility to celebrate the achievements of the past and also to call out the problems that persist; collections such as the Baldwin Library are not static collections but rather dynamic, ongoing sites of cultural valuation and analysis.

We hope you enjoy and learn from this alphabet tour of the Baldwin Library of Historical Children's Literature. And we invite you to visit!

▶ ***Pinocchio,*** by Carlo Collodi, illustrated by Frederick Richardson, published by John C. Winston Company (c.1923).

▲ ***"Finger Play*** & ***Monday, St. Nicholas Magazine,*** by Edith Goodyear Alger (1895).

B is for Baldwin

An Alphabet Tour of the Baldwin Library of Historical Children's Literature

▲ ***On the Way to Wonderland,*** by Clara Doty Bates, published by D. Lothrop & Co. (c.1885).

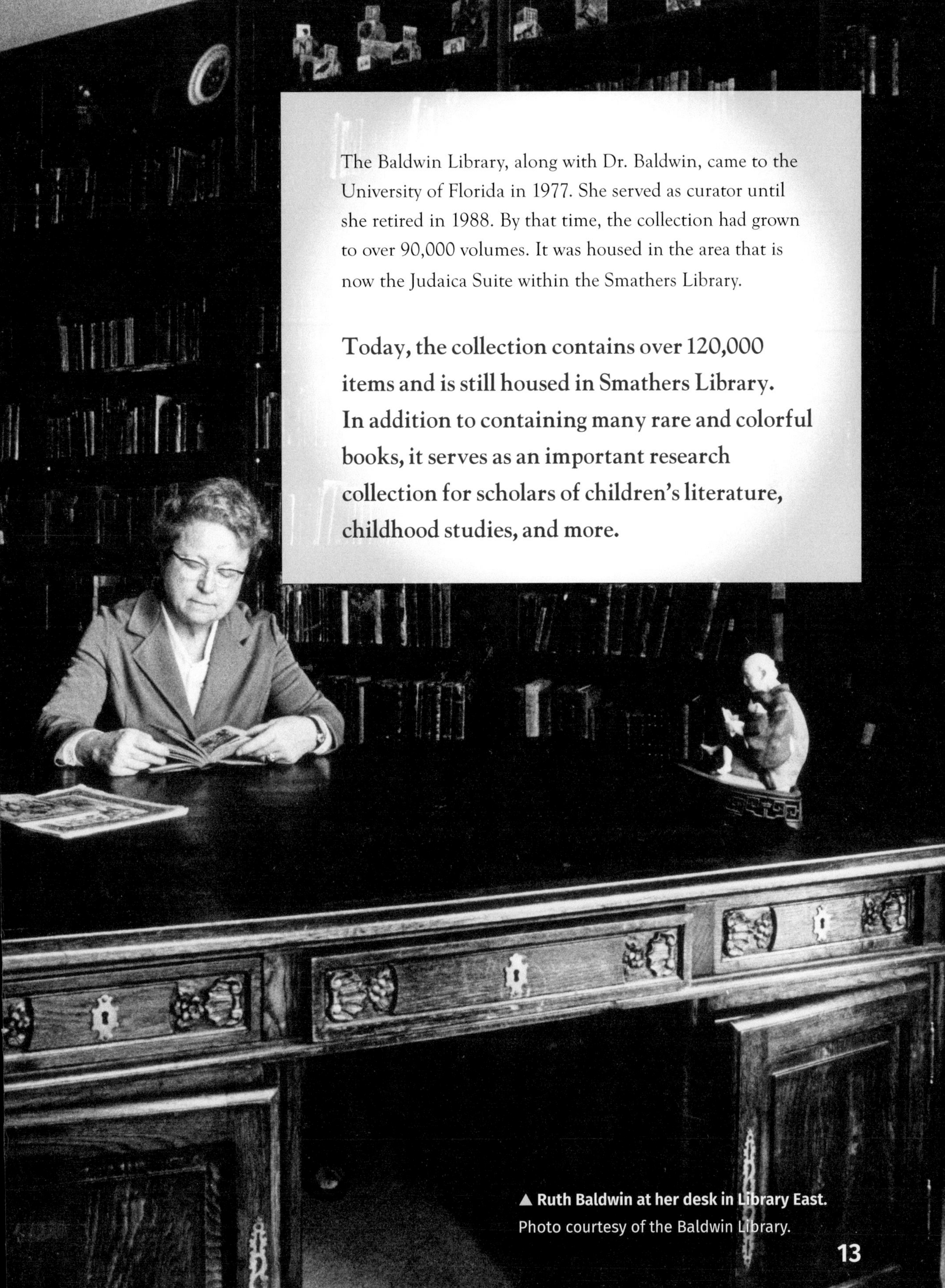

The Baldwin Library, along with Dr. Baldwin, came to the University of Florida in 1977. She served as curator until she retired in 1988. By that time, the collection had grown to over 90,000 volumes. It was housed in the area that is now the Judaica Suite within the Smathers Library.

Today, the collection contains over 120,000 items and is still housed in Smathers Library. In addition to containing many rare and colorful books, it serves as an important research collection for scholars of children's literature, childhood studies, and more.

▲ Ruth Baldwin at her desk in Library East.
Photo courtesy of the Baldwin Library.

► ***Little Lucy's Wonderful Globe,***
by Charlotte Mary Yonge,
Illustrated by Lorenz Frølich,
published by D. Lothrop & Co.
and G.T. Day & Co. (1872).

A is for Anglophone

Anuja Madan

An important project of British children's literature in the 19th century was to promote the imperial work of the British Empire.

A range of religious tracts, geographical and historical primers, adventure stories and travel narratives sought to acquaint young Britons with its colonial territories and their populations, establish British cultural and political supremacy, and train boy readers into becoming future imperial masters.

NATIVE WOMAN OF BENGAL.

▲ ***Adventures of Two Youths in a Journey to Ceylon and India,*** by Thomas Wallace Knox, published by Harper & Brothers (1882).

Tracts such as Amos Sutton's *The Hindu Foundling Girl* (1834) and Rev. Alexander Duff's *Charlotte the Hindoo Orphan and Other Tales from the East* (1877) portray Hindu children as abject subjects in need of rescue. Duff credited missionary schools with enlightening Hindu girls, who are "mostly left to grow up in ignorance" (90). In this popular tract, converted Hindu girls exemplify Christian piety for young readers. Tracts also aimed to influence young minds towards missionary work, as in Henry Standing's *The Children of Madagascar* (1887), which was written to "draw out the sympathy of [his] boy and girl readers towards their brothers and sisters in this island and increase their interest in the great mission work which is being done here" (5). After 1825, tracts about colonies included those published by American religious organizations such as the American Sunday-School Union, including the popular, *Letters to Sabbath School Children on the Condition of the Heathen* (1843) and *Life of Christian F. Swartz, an Early Missionary in India* (1830).

Also meant to instruct young British and American children were a number of women-authored books sometimes written in the guise of fiction in order to instill information about the colonies. From Priscilla Wakefield's

MRS. JUDSON TEACHING A CLASS OF NATIVE CONVERTS.

▲ ***Adventures of Two Youths in a Journey to Ceylon and India,*** by Thomas Wallace Knox, published by Harper & Brothers (1882).

A

GEOGRAPHICAL PRESENT;

BEING

Descriptions

OF

THE PRINCIPAL COUNTRIES

OF

THE WORLD.

BY MARY ANNE VENNING.

SECOND EDITION.

LONDON:

PRINTED FOR DARTON, HARVEY, AND DARTON, GRACECHURCH-STREET.

1818.

Man & Woman of Ceylon.

▲ ***Adventures of Two Youths in a Journey to Ceylon and India,*** by Thomas Wallace Knox, published by Harper & Brothers (1882).

enormously successful Arthur Middleton travel series (*A Family Tour of the British Empire, Excursions in North America, Traveller in Africa*, and *Traveller in Asia),* and Charlotte Mary Yonge's *Little Lucy's Wonderful Globe* to the little-known works of Mary Anne Venning (*A Geographical Present)* and Mary Boscawen (*Conversations on Geography),* tarry-at-home travelers were encouraged to read their way through the Empire. These texts were often simultaneously anthropological, historical, and geographical as many included maps that charted colonial territory. Often, the boundaries between primers and tracts were blurred, as in William Stone's *My First Voyage: A Book for*

tions of the various Inhabitants in their
respective Costumes,

Man & Woman of Hindostan.

Man & Woman of Goa.

Man & Woman of Constantinople.

◀ ***A Geographical Present,*** by Mary Anne Venning (1818).

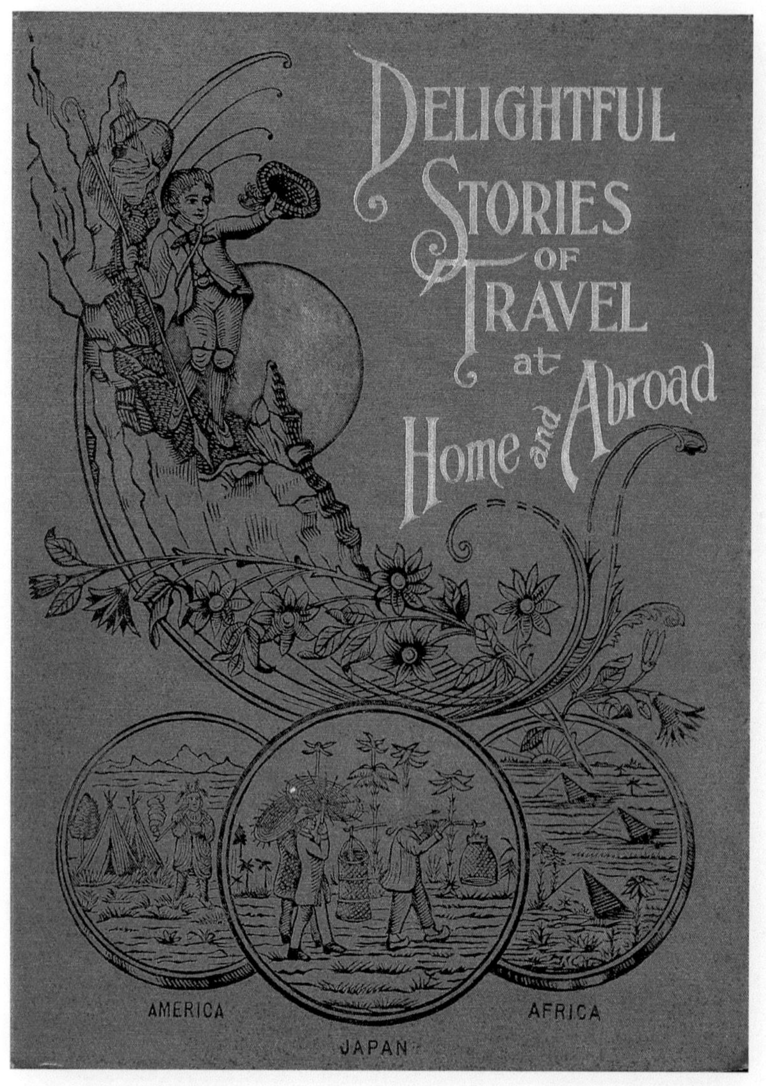

▲ ***Delightful Stories of Travel at Home and Abroad,*** by Allen E. Fowler, published by World Bible House (1895).

Youth (1860), which ends with two chapters titled "Old Times—Heathendom—the Feast of the Dead" and "New Times—the Missionary."

Travel narratives were published by many American authors too. Popular writers such as Thomas Knox (*The Boy Travelers on the Congo*, 1887; *Adventures of Two Youths in a Journey to Ceylon and India*, 1882; *Adventures of Two Youths in a Journey Through Africa*, 1884) and William Taylor Adams/Oliver Optic (All-Over-the-World Library series) featured boy characters and targeted boy readers. These texts demonstrated an assumption of complete mastery over the East. Adams writes in his *Four Young Explorers or Sight-Seeing in the Tropics* (1896) that "this book contains all one need to know about Borneo" (viii). The reinforcement of Orientalist stereotypes was a common theme. Talking about the Dyak tribe, one of the characters states that the Dyaks have "almost as many inferior deities as the Hindus" and that "they are very superstitious" (89). Histories of these civilizations invariably touch upon the "primitivism" and "barbarism" of their past. In Allen E. Fowler's *Delightful Stories of Travel at Home and Abroad* (1895), we are told that "the Pyramids raise their head high in the air, a silent testimony to despotic power, for sublime as they are, they were built by slaves under the master's lash, an unwilling offering to the sway of Kings . . . Could [the Sphinx] but speak, what a tale of sorrow, of suffering, of the miseries of the old civilization it would tell" (21).

◀ ***Adventures of Two Youths in a Journey to Ceylon and India with descriptions of Borneo, the Philippine Islands and Burmah,*** by Thomas Wallace Knox, published by Harper & Brothers (1882).

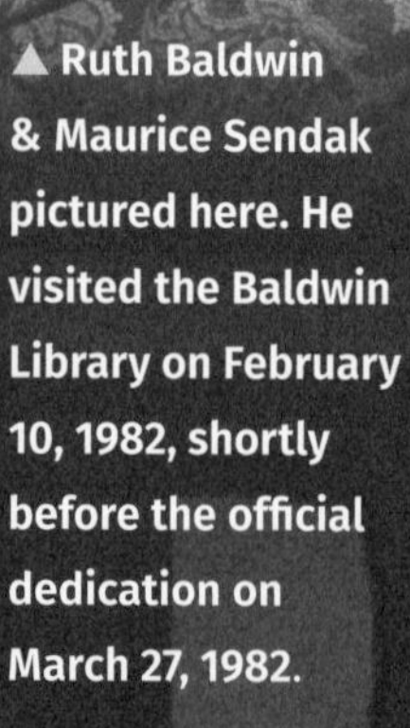

▲ Ruth Baldwin & Maurice Sendak pictured here. He visited the Baldwin Library on February 10, 1982, shortly before the official dedication on March 27, 1982.

This article is in an abridgement of Rita Smith's original article, "Caught Up in the Whirlwind: Ruth Baldwin." ***The Lion and the Unicorn, 22:3*** **(1998).** Reprinted with permission of Johns Hopkins University Press.

Rita Smith

I first met Ruth Baldwin briefly in 1977 when I worked for a year in the Acquisitions Department of the University of Florida Library.

is for Baldwin

I met her a second time one Saturday when I had a garage sale, and she stopped in for about thirty seconds to look through my box of children's books. I met her a third time when I walked over to the Baldwin Library unannounced, introduced myself, and said I was looking for a job. I knew very little about her. She was a stocky woman of medium height, seventy years old with steely gray hair, a wide forehead, a solid stance, and a determined set to her mouth. She sized me up and during the next hour proceeded to show me part of her collection of children's books: pop-ups and transformations from the nineteenth century, shelves of books by G. A. Henty, an entire cabinet of hundreds of chapbooks, complete runs of nineteenth-century children's periodicals, and a book of children's stories with original woodcuts by Alexander Anderson. This tour was accompanied by a recitation of her problems since bringing the collection to the University of Florida, a recitation spiked with a dry, sardonic sense of humor and punctuated by short bursts of laughter. The position was just what I didn't want: full-time, permanent, and nonprofessional, but I was awed by the collection and intrigued by Baldwin. I took the job when it was offered to me.

▶ Photos courtesy of the Baldwin Library.

Baldwin was born on September 29, 1918 on a farm outside of Due West, South Carolina. After several brief stays in small college towns, the family settled in Urbana, Illinois where her father, Professor Thomas Baldwin, had accepted a faculty position in the English department at the University of Illinois. She grew up in Urbana along with her two younger sisters. After high school, she attended Muskingum College in New Concord, Ohio, and received a bachelor's degree in 1939. Over the next fifteen years she attended the University of Illinois between jobs to earn her bachelor's and master's degrees, and finally, in December 1955, her doctorate in Library Science. In January 1956, Louisiana State University hired her as a faculty member of the School of Library Science. She taught there for twenty-one years, not children's or young adult literature, however, as one might expect, but library management.

Baldwin began collecting things as a child. One dresser in the attic of the Baldwin house in Urbana was labeled "Ruth's Museum," and it held great treasures including arrowheads, rattlesnake rattles, rocks, shells, seeds, and nuts. When the seeds and nuts produced worms that invaded the attic, they had to go, but the collections of arrowheads, rocks, and shells stayed and grew and were joined over the years by collections of stamps, Fu dogs, buttons, boot hooks, elephant statues, rabbit tails, jewelry, postmarks, Roosevelt dimes, and, of course, beginning in the fall of 1953, the children's

◀ **Assorted Chapbooks.**

Photo courtesy of the Baldwin Library.

books that soon became the focus of her collecting interests.

Baldwin turned thirty-five in September of that year. She was living in her parents' house in Urbana working on her doctorate. Her parents were on sabbatical in England, and, as a birthday present, they sent her a bundle of forty children's chapbooks. Her mother had found them while browsing in Mcleush's Bookstore, and her father agreed that they would make a good birthday present for Ruth. Baldwin, with her proclivity for collecting things, which she described as her "magpie instinct," took a lively interest in the books, and her mother continued to send children's books when she found them. By the time the Christmas holidays were over, both Baldwin and her mother were hooked.

In the beginning, Baldwin didn't have a grand scheme for building a library. She didn't think she had the funds or the time to do anything much with children's books, but after that first year, she admitted later to Gillian Avery, she "got caught up in the whirlwind." She may never have elaborated a grand scheme for her collection, but she knew from the beginning that she was collecting to build a library for scholars. She wanted books that children had actually read and handled, and although over the years she acquired first editions of all but a few classics, she was not looking for them. In a speech given in 1982, Baldwin suggested that the library was "a wonderful research repository for social historians, scientists, theologians, geographers, philosophers, and other specialists interested in a popular explanation and understanding of almost anything in which children were involved in the late eighteenth, nineteenth, and early twentieth centuries." Baldwin was of the opinion that the books that children read were often not the books libraries would have for them.

This collecting philosophy dovetailed nicely with her financial situation. It always irritated her when someone said, "I wish I had money to buy a library like yours." She never had much money and for many years lived from paycheck to paycheck. Her salary from LSU was her only income, supplemented by her parents when they were able to do so. Eventually, especially after her move to the University of Florida, she did spend more on books as she tried to fill the nineteenth-century gaps, and she pursued specific publications such as those of the American Tract Society. She budgeted her income very carefully and often went without things she wanted in order to buy books. Her greatest financial challenge was managing to stay solvent, thanks to some financial help from her father, after the purchase of $20,000 worth of pre-1820 American imprints and nineteenth-century alphabets from Benjamin Tighe, a Massachusetts book dealer.

Once she began the collection, every trip, every excursion she took—whether it was a trip to Cleveland to visit her sister, or a trip to Due West to visit relatives, or a trip to New York job hunting—became a book-hunting trip, even though that was not its primary purpose. In October 1955, for example, she and her mother drove to New York. Baldwin was job hunting, not book hunting, but in her notes she doesn't mention the jobs she looked for or the interviews she may have had. She does mention stopping at Lionel Swicker's Old Book Store in Akron, Ohio, and buying fifty books for $24.25. She mentions stopping in Cleveland to visit her sister and creeping downtown in heavy rain to find books at the Goodwill and Salvation Army. When she moved to Baton Rouge in January 1956, she had purchased over one thousand nineteenth-century children's books.

Baldwin took her first trip to England in the early 1960s with the English-Speaking Union of New Orleans. It was only incidentally a book-buying trip, but it offered her a vision of the opportunities for buying books there. She returned the following summer specifically to visit used book dealers. Planning to finance her English purchases by selling the duplicates once she returned to the States, she had decided she was going to buy every nineteenth-century book for children that children had actually read and handled that she could find and that wasn't too expensive (that is, no more than a pound or two). She accomplished this, as indicated in a letter to friends: "Because I wanted to spend as little time selecting books as possible, I made a clean sweep and bought everything everywhere under two pounds which fit my collection regardless."

This second trip to England was a very rewarding experience, as Baldwin purchased over 1,500 books for her collection. Later that fall, when all the books arrived in Baton Rouge and were put out on shelves, she looked at them and wrote to her parents, "I have to admit that last night when I got the last book from the last package on the shelves and the last shelf respaced—well, it makes you kind of numb. [It's] like a great masterpiece." She continued making annual trips to England for many years. Eventually book dealers held books for her throughout the year, awaiting her arrival, and over the years she developed many friendships and contacts among the English book sellers.

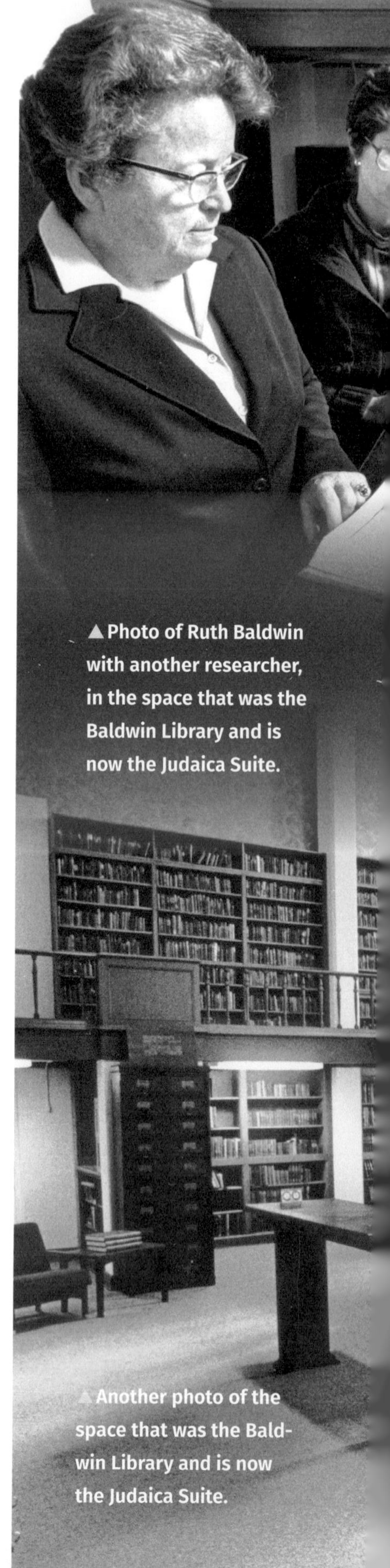

▲ Photo of Ruth Baldwin with another researcher, in the space that was the Baldwin Library and is now the Judaica Suite.

▲ Another photo of the space that was the Baldwin Library and is now the Judaica Suite.

Photos courtesy of the Baldwin Library.

By the mid-1970s, Baldwin had moved to a bigger house and built a room on the back to accommodate her expanding library. She could not afford to insure it and began to worry about losing it through theft, fire, or hurricane. She started looking for a suitable institution for her collection, which included hiring her as curator. In 1975, Professor Joy Anderson of the English department at the University of Florida visited Baton Rouge to give a lecture on children's literature. She learned about Dr. Baldwin's library and was invited to have a look at it.

Browsing through the collection, Professor Anderson realized what a rich resource it would be for scholars interested in the historical, cultural, social, and literary aspects of children's literature. Upon returning to Florida, Anderson spoke of the collection to the head of the English department, Dr. Ward Hellstrom, and to the director of the university library, Dr. Gustav Harrer. Harrer and Hellstrom flew to Baton Rouge to see the collection for themselves and expressed a keen interest in having the collection moved to Florida. Baldwin appreciated the interest, but she wasn't sure if Florida was the place for her collection. "It was a nice experience," she noted in a letter to a group of friends.

> I haven't been wooed that much in this life not to appreciate it, but I honestly have no idea whether that is where I will go. I do not know that the University as a whole is strong enough to support this project in the way they say they are willing to do and the way I would insist upon. On the other hand I don't know that any southern university is, and if I wait for "Mr. Exactly Right" I'll probably be right here until I die.

In spite of her misgivings, Baldwin donated her collection of 35,000 nineteenth-century children's books to the University of Florida in 1977.

After the move to Florida, Baldwin decided that a great research library of historical children's literature should not end with the nineteenth century, so she began to collect twentieth-century books as well, concentrating on books published before 1950. She now had university funds with which to purchase books, as well as her own salary, a substantial sum from the sale of her father's personal library to the University of Illinois, and her own book sales. She began scouring the territory around Gainesville.

▼***Alice's Adventures in Wonderland,*** by Lewis Carroll, Illustrated by Blanche McManus, published by M. F. Mansfield and A. Wessels (c.1899).

Many scholars have used the resources found in the Baldwin Library. Gillian Avery conducted much of the research for *Behold the Child, American Children and Their Books, 1621–1922*, at the Baldwin Library. In an interview after the publication of that book, Avery said:

> *Behold the Child* was written because, when I asked Ruth Baldwin . . . what was the best reference book . . . on the subject of American children's books, supposing that there was at least a score, she said, "well actually there aren't any," and I was so fascinated by the contents of her library and the American books sitting side by side by the English that I thought, why couldn't I have a try.

A graduate student at the University of Florida has discovered that Mrs. Henry Wood, who wrote highly romantic sensational books for adults during the 1860s, also wrote school stories for children and has done research comparing her books for adults with those for children. Baldwin's own publication, *100 Nineteenth Century Rhyming Alphabets in English*, draws examples from the Victorian alphabets she bought from Ben Tighe. Lawrence Darton reviewed over three hundred books with the Darton imprint for a history and bibliography of publisher William Darton and his successors.

Richard Wunderlich utilized the extensive Pinnocchio collection held by the Baldwin Library in his bibliography, *The Pinnocchio Catalogue: being a descriptive bibliography and printing history of English language translations . . . 1892–1987.*

In discussing qualities needed to build a book collection that other people could utilize and enjoy, Gillian Avery said:

> It goes far beyond persistence and single-mindedness. . . . You need patience, consistency, a superb memory, remorseless attention to detail, yet an ability to detach yourself from detail and to visualize the whole, a beautifully-ordered mind, imagination, flair, and . . . luck.

Photos courtesy of the Baldwin Library.

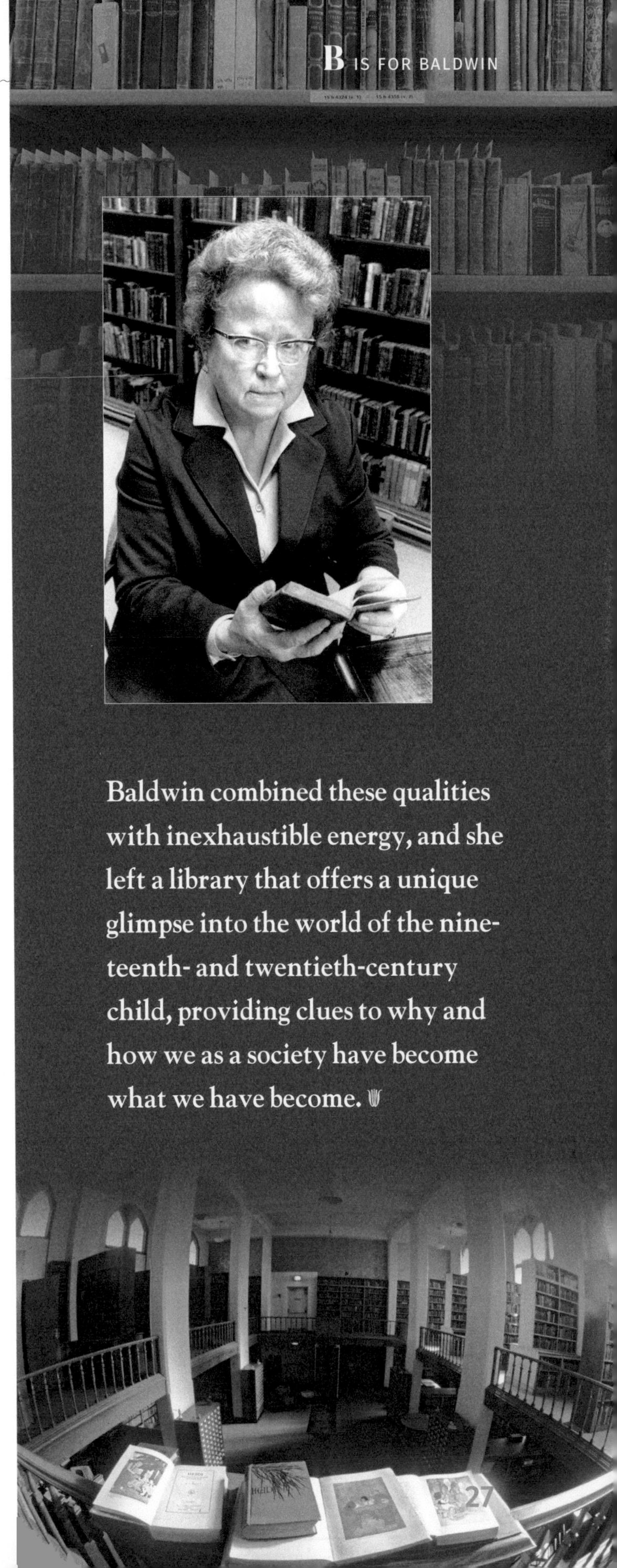

Baldwin combined these qualities with inexhaustible energy, and she left a library that offers a unique glimpse into the world of the nineteenth- and twentieth-century child, providing clues to why and how we as a society have become what we have become.

▲ ***A New History of Blue Beard,*** by Gaffer Black Beard, published by John Adams (1804).

▲ ***Book About Animals,*** by Rufus Merrill, illustrated, published by Rufus Merrill (1850).

15

as the rats and mice were devouring that also. He immediately put down puss, who killed a great part of them, and the rest ran away.

The king having seen the wonderful exploits of Mrs. Puss, and being informed that she was with young, and would furnish the whole country, bargained with the

▲ ***Whittington and His Cat,*** by Sidney's Press, published by John Babcock and Son & S. Babcock & Co. (1824).

Robert Thomson

Chapbook is the name generally afforded to those small unbound and uncut but folded sheets that were sold by itinerant hawkers or "chapmen" to the population at large.

is for Chapbook

They were often formed into 16, 24 or 32 paged texts and if more than a single sheet was used, they could be gathered into books with only a paper wrapper to contain the contents—no glue, no stitching and no staples; John Kendrew of York's edition of the *Robin Hood's Garland* (1770) is an example that ran to 108 pages within its blue paper wrapper.

The widest possible range of subject matter was covered by these ephemeral publications indicating that the intended audience was as diverse as the printers could conceive. Thus we encounter prognostications, prophecies and explanations for dreams; religious and moral guides or warnings to encourage proper conduct; household manuals from cook books to ABCs for the children and, no doubt, other new readers; historical and political events of note; geographical travels and adventures; prose and verse fictions including legendary romances, fairy stories and other folk tales; song books, nursery rhymes and jests; and so the various categories continue. By the turn of the nineteenth/twentieth century, large collections had been accumulated by libraries and individual antiquarians. One such gathering at Harvard University was expertly catalogued in 1906 with deputy librarian Tillinghast's classification. This taxonomy has since been edited by Victor Neuberg (*Chapbooks*, London, 1979) into 23 distinct categories and provides us with the most satisfactory arrangement yet developed.

The chapbook collection in the Baldwin Library contains examples of nearly all the categories, though of course with Ruth Baldwin's emphasis upon children's reading and readers, the predominant texts are legendary romances, fairy stories and folktales in both prose and verse with the addition of many works of moral suasion for young minds. In many cases, Baldwin gathered multiple editions of the same texts by printers on both sides of the Atlantic. This is particularly true of the extensive coverage of folk stories by Perrault and others that were translated into English in the early eighteenth century and frequently reprinted thereafter. Of particular interest are the many editions of *Jack and the Giants, Jack the Giant Killer, Jack and the Beanstalk,* and also the many iterations of Cinderella or "Cinderilla" as it is often found. *Tom Thumb, Sleeping Beauty* and also *The Children in the Wood* with its much less common sequel, *The Children in the Wood Restored*, or, *The Hermit of the Forest* were all clearly good sellers throughout Britain and the Eastern seaboard of North America.

▲ ***New ABC,*** by Isaiah Thomas, published by I. Thomas, Jun. (1805).

◀ ***Little Verses for Good Children,*** by J. Metcalf (1840).

Among the major American printers active in the late eighteenth and early nineteenth centuries, the Baldwin collection has large numbers of titles printed by Isaiah Thomas and later, his son in Boston; Nathaniel Coverly and later members of his family in Boston; J. Babcock, and J. Babcock and Son, Hartford. British printers appear to be well covered from 1750 to 1860 or thereabouts. In particular, very large numbers of chapbooks from J.G. Rusher of Banbury are in the collection as individual chapbooks and also gathered together and bound up in one volume, as was the custom of Samuel Pepys in the seventeenth century. There are also a large number of Scottish chapbooks "Printed for the Booksellers"—perhaps the work of Glasgow printers James Lumsden and Son who specialized in legendary tales, fairy stories, and folktales often in verse.

16

XERXES.

Xerxes in all his pomp and state,
Did like an infant cry,
To think his host, so vast, so great,
In one poor age must die.

U V W X

▲ ***Pleasing Toy,*** by J. Metcalf (1835).

There are, of course, rare items, seldom encountered in any other collection. For instance, the cautionary tale *The Prodigal Daughter*, printed by Zachariah Fowle in Boston around 1760-1770. It bears a large woodcut on the title page which shows the daughter rising from her bed—or is it her coffin? The identical chapbook, text and woodcut, is found printed by Fowle's former (indentured 1755) apprentice, Isaiah Thomas in the early 1770s about the time Thomas took over his ex Master's business—a copy is in the Rosenbach collection. Isaiah Thomas has replaced Fowle's imprint with his own but otherwise the two editions appear identical, thus demonstrating a wonderful example of the continuity of trade—from master to apprentice turned journeyman.

Another rare example is the common chapbook *Cinderella and Her Glass Slipper* printed by Orlando Hodgson in London circa 1835. This edition has a fold-out plate of some eight cells of comic-like storytelling all brightly hand-colored.

An altogether more serious item that is exceedingly rare is the chapbook printed for Francis Westley in 1825, *Pity the Negro, or, An Address to Children on the Subject of Slavery*. The Baldwin copy is the third printing with a paper wrapper around it bearing the title page of a fourth edition. It will be remembered that 1825 sees the beginning of the first Anti-Slavery Society founded by William Wilberforce and Thomas Clarkson. Though the trading in slaves had been banned by the British Parliament in 1807, it was not until 1833 that slavery itself was supposedly abolished—in fact, it was to be some five years before the abolishment was effective throughout the then British colonies. This chapbook focuses in particular upon the situation in Jamaica, St. Croix and Barbados. Pages 13-15 highlight their misery by reprinting notices from Kingston, Jamaica newspapers of runaway slaves and recaptured slaves held in St. George's Workhouse on June 10, 1823.

Including various religious and Cheap Repository-styled chapbooks of moral suasion, there are perhaps around two thousand true chapbooks in the Baldwin Library. These offer egress to a wide range of research topics and deserve close scrutiny.

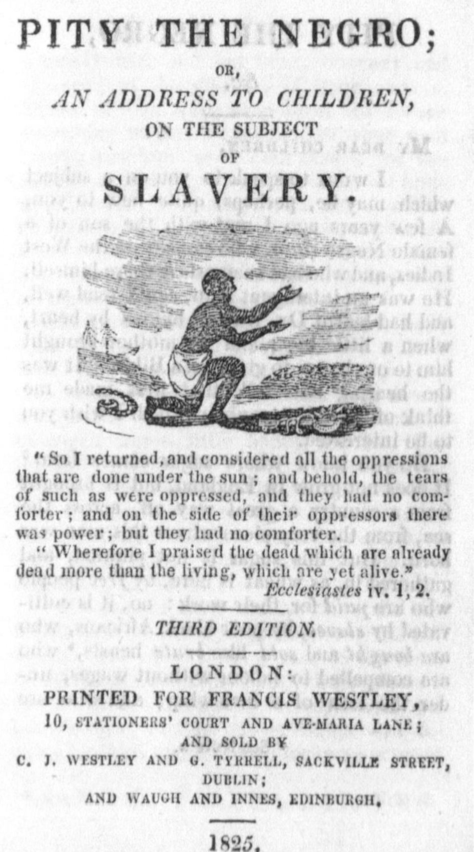

PITY THE NEGRO;

OR,

AN ADDRESS TO CHILDREN,

ON THE SUBJECT

OF

SLAVERY.

"So I returned, and considered all the oppressions that are done under the sun; and behold, the tears of such as were oppressed, and they had no comforter; and on the side of their oppressors there was power; but they had no comforter.

"Wherefore I praised the dead which are already dead more than the living, which are yet alive."

Ecclesiastes iv. 1, 2.

THIRD EDITION.

LONDON:

PRINTED FOR FRANCIS WESTLEY,

10, STATIONERS' COURT AND AVE-MARIA LANE;

AND SOLD BY

C. J. WESTLEY AND G. TYRRELL, SACKVILLE STREET, DUBLIN;

AND WAUGH AND INNES, EDINBURGH.

1825.

▲ ***Pity the Negro, Or, An Address to Children on the Subject of Slavery,*** by Francis Westley, published for Francis Westley (1825).

Cinderella scolded by her Mother in Law.
Cinderella's dismay at finding her Clothes & Equipage
CINDERELLA
quipage Changed.)
The Ball.
(Surprise of the Sisters on se
The Fairy her Godmother effecting the Change.
the Sisters on seeing that the Glass Slipp

▲ ***History of Cinderella and Her Glass Slipper,*** printed by Orlando Hodgson (c.1835).

▲ ***We Are Seven,*** by William Wordsworth, illustrated by Agnes Gardner King, published by Meissner & Buch (1892?).

◀ ***Religious Experience and Death of Eliza Van Wyck,*** published by the American Tract Society (1830-1832).

is for Death

Kristen Gregory

When I was asked to design a course on the Baldwin Library, I knew I wanted to theme it on death.

In much of contemporary Western society, death has become increasingly forbidden as childhood has become increasingly sacred, and thus it is rare to find a space devoted to both childhood and death. The Baldwin Library is obviously a space of childhood. However, as much as the collection embodies childhood, it also evokes death. Death haunts the texts in the scribblings in the margins and the dust on the pages, which remind us of the children who once held these volumes. The collection also includes a variety of children's literature on death, including Puritan religious tracts, Romantic poetry, fairy tales, and Gorey's macabre works.

The Baldwin holds an immense collection of Puritan texts, the most notable of which are James Janeway's *A Token for Children* and *The New England Primer*. Due to high child mortality rates and strict religious convictions, Puritans did not shield their children from death. They needed to be saved from their innate sinfulness, and death was the ultimate scare tactic. For example, one edition of *A Token for Children* questions the child reader, "How do you know but that you may be the next child to die" (xi)? And *The New England Primer* includes its notoriously ominous alphabet rhyme with entries like "While Youth do cheer, Death may be near." The Baldwin also houses hundreds of lesser-known children's memorials, which record the deathbed conversions of children as young as three years old. In these texts, children cannot be protected from death, so the threat of death is used to protect them from vice.

THE
PRODIGAL DAUGHTER:
BEING
A ſtrange and wonder Relation of a young Lady in *Briſtol*, who, becauſe her Parents would not ſupport her in her Extravagance, bargained with the Devil to poiſon them --- How an Angel informed her Parents of her Deſign.----How ſhe lay in a Trance four Days.---- How ſhe came to Life again, &c, &c.-----Likewiſe the Subſtance of a Sermon on this Occaſion, from *Luke* xv. 24.

Printed and Sold in *Back-ſtreet*, BOSTON.

▲ ***The Prodigal Daughter,*** by Sidney Babcock, printed by Zachariah Fowles (1767).

In contrast to these Puritan texts, the Baldwin also contains books that romanticize death in childhood. In Wordsworth's "We are Seven," an adult narrator tries to convince a young girl that her dead siblings are gone, but she repeatedly answers that they are still here. The poem is accompanied by beautiful illustrations of the girl eating and playing next to her siblings' gravestones. The poem romanticizes the dead children as the girl reminds us that they are not gone but still accompany her. This fantasy of the dead child as forever innocent (and perfect) also appears in tales like "The Little Match Girl," "Babes in the Wood," and *Peter and Wendy*. The Baldwin's various illustrated editions of these texts highlight the connection between the romanticized dead child and the forever child.

Of the 31 Edward Gorey texts in the Baldwin, *Gashlycrumb Tinies and The Dwindling Party* most clearly center death. *Gashlycrumb Tinies* recants the brutal deaths of 26 children in an alphabet rhyme. While the format of

Gashlycrumb Tinies mirrors Puritan primers, the grisly violence recalls earlier fairy tales, like The Grimms' "The Juniper Tree," in which a stepmother decapitates her stepson and feeds him in a stew to her family. Gorey reminds us that death has always been a part of children's literature, but rather than use it to instruct or romanticize children, Gorey enables child readers to play along and laugh at the concept of death. For example, one of my students noted that his movable picture book, *The Dwindling Party*, invites the child reader to be complicit in the murders, as s/he pulls each tab that kills one of the family members. In Gorey's work, death is neither feared nor romantic, and the child reader is empowered to play in response to death.

These are only a few of the texts on death in the Baldwin, but this brief survey provides us with a chance to reflect on the powerful effects of death and childhood on the cultural imagination, and explore the role that children's literature plays in the formation, critique, continuation, and revision of our ever-shifting values and anxieties.

And in a voyage to Portugal
Two of his sonnes did dye;
And to conclude, himselfe was brought
To want and miserye.

He pawn'd and mortgaged all his land,
Ere seven yeares came about.
And now at length this wicked act
Did by this meanes come out.

The fellowe, that did take in hand
These children for to kill,
Was for a robbery judg'd to dye,
Such was God's blessed will:

Who did confess the very truth,
As here hath been display'd:
Their uncle having dyed in gaol,
Where he for debt was layd.

You that executors be made,
And overseers eke
Of children that be fatherless,
And infants mild and meek,

Take you example by this thing,
And yield to each his right,
Lest God with such like miserye
Your wicked minds requite.

Lithographed in Colors by John Brandard and Printed by M. & N. Hanhart, London.

▲ ***Babes in the Wood,*** printed by William Dickes, published by Sampson, Low, Son & Co. (1861).

▶ ***Banbury Cross & Other Nursery Rhymes,*** illustrated by Alice B. Woodward, published by J. M. Dent & Co. (1893).

▲ ***Robinson Crusoe Picture Book,*** by Daniel Defoe, published by George Routledge and Sons (c.1870).

▶ ***The Boy's Book of Inventions,*** by Ray Stannard, Baker, published by Doubleday & McClure Co. (1899).

Anastasia Ulanowicz

What constitutes an education, and what does it mean to be educated?

is for Education

▲ ***Robinson Crusoe Picture Book,*** by Daniel Defoe, published by George Routledge and Sons (c.1870).

Does an education imply a young person's satisfactory demonstration of institutionally required cognitive skills, or does it rather involve her internalization of culturally proscribed moral values? Is an educated person one who has assimilated the information received through a specific pedagogical tradition, or is an individual whose experience has taught one to question and critique received knowledge?

Conventionally, education is associated with schooling, and surely the *New England Primer* is an icon of the early American pedagogical tradition. Originally published in 1687 by the English émigré-printer Benjamin Harris and reproduced by several publishers throughout the nineteenth century, the *Primer* is an anthology of prayers, sermons, catechisms, vocabulary lists, and renditions of an illustrated alphabet that famously begins with the verse, "In Adam's fall/We sinned all." Each version of the *Primer* housed in the Baldwin is a diminutive text—no larger than 3x5 inches—evidently designed for little hands. The pocket-sized dimensions of these books suggest their intended portability on, or close to, the reader's own body. Indeed, their very form concretizes an admonition offered in the 1840 edition published by S.A. Howland: "My book and Heart/Shall never part."

If the *New England Primer* has long preoccupied historians of childhood and education, this is in part because it makes visible substantial cultural shifts in thinking about the intellectual, moral, and psychological capacities of young people. For instance, each edition's vocabulary list includes abstract and multisyllabic words—among them, "formidably," "damnify," "edification," "abomination"—that today would seem hardly appropriate for young readers. Likewise, the *Primer* includes graphic images of illness and death from which contemporary children are largely shielded: it does not refrain from illustrating, for example, a boil-pocked Job resting ever-patiently on a dung-heap, Rachel's grief over her first-born children, or the 1554 execution of Protestant martyr John Rogers. Even so, successive editions of the *Primer* demonstrate a gradual softening of attitudes toward young pupils. In the revised alphabet published in the mid-nineteenth-century Howland edition (1840s), for instance, "C" and "D" no longer stand for Christ's crucifixion and the "Deluge" faced by Noah, respectively, but rather for familiar domestic creatures, the cat and dog. Likewise, "M" no longer stands for the Mosaic Law, but is rather employed to impart a surprisingly consoling message: "The Moon gives light/In time of night."

▲ ***Cherry Stones,*** by William Adams, illustrated by Tompkins Harrison Matteson, published by General Protestant Episcopal Sunday School Union (1851).

Schoolbooks such as the *Primer*, however, only offer a partial perspective on shifting cultural and historical notions of childhood education. The literary tradition of the "school story" provides scholars further insight into how young people experienced schooling—and in turn, how the adults they became reconciled such experiences with the ideological values they internalized throughout the course of their education. Traditionally, the emergence of the school story genre is marked by the 1857 publication of Thomas Hughes' *Tom Brown's School Days*, which was inspired by the author's own experiences at Rugby. Intriguingly, at least one school story contained in the Baldwin Library predates *Tom Brown's School Days*, and thus calls scholars to consider the possible influences of literary antecedents on Hughes' foundational novel. William Adams' *The Cherry Stones—Or, the Charlton School: A Tale For Youth* (1852) features a top-performing British schoolboy-protagonist, Harry Mertoun, whose virtue is compromised when he steals fruit from a neighboring orchard. Ultimately, Harry's headmaster discerns the cause of his guilt and administers a just punishment. Thus, *The Cherry Stones*, much like later and better-known school stories, depicts the school as the site of not only intellectual but also moral education.

Of course, education—be it intellectual or moral—need not occur within the institutional confines of the school. Indeed, Daniel Defoe's *Robinson Crusoe* (1719) has long been

NEW ENGLAND PRIMER. 19

MR. JOHN RODGERS, minister of the gospel, in London, was the first martyr in Queen Mary's reign, and was burnt at Smithfield, Feb. 14th, 1554. His wife, with nine small children, and one at her breast, followed him to the stake; with which sorrowful sight he was not in the least daunted, but with wonderful patience, died courageously for the gospel of JESUS CHRIST.

Some few days before his death, he wrote the follow ing Advice to his Children.

Give ear, my children, to my words,
Whom God hath dearly bought;

▲▼ ***New England Primer, Improved,*** printed by Sidney Babcock (between 1826-1830).

NEW ENGLAND PRIMER. 11

As runs the *Glass*,
Man's life doth pass.

My *Book* and *Heart*,
Shall never part.

Job feels the Rod,
Yet blesses GOD.

Proud *Korah's* troop,
Was swallowed up.

The *Lion* bold,
The *Lamb* doth hold.

The *Moon* gives light,
In time of night.

A 6

celebrated, most famously by Jean-Jacques Rousseau, as a model of education earned through direct experience. *The Robinson Crusoe Picture Book*, published in 1870 by George Routledge and Sons, offers 24 lushly colored illustrations that draw the reader's attention to an ideal, "natural" education: the hero's inventive repurposing of found objects on his desert island; his domestication of native species; and his use of inductive reasoning in discerning the presence of his eventual helpmate, Friday, from footprints in the sand.

If, however, *The Robinson Crusoe Picture Book* functions as a literal illustration of education that is radically separated from institutionalized learning, some of its supplementary materials comment on more traditional forms of knowledge acquisition. Appended to this picture book is a collection of poems entitled "Queer Characters," which feature anthropomorphized animals going about quotidian human activities. In one of these poems, "Doctor Donkey's Academy," a mere beast of burden takes on the "worthy" task of instructing his fellow creatures. On the one hand, the poem explicitly celebrates its hero's characteristically mulish stubbornness: his "patience" is a "virtue" that "goes further than his knowledge" and thus ultimately allows him to earn the respect of his young animal-scholars. On the other hand, however, the poem implicitly mocks the intellectual dullness of educational environments presided by dim but well-intended instructors who favor desultory lessons over independent creative engagement. In this way, the text subtly prompts the reader to question the ultimate purpose of education: is it intended to produce a well-disciplined sense of moral virtue, or is it rather designed to foster critical acuity? Certainly, the many children's texts contained within the Baldwin invite scholars to consider how this question has been variously posed and answered over three centuries of Anglo-American history.

▲ ***Picture Book of Florida,*** by Bernadine Bailey, illustrated by, Kurt Wiese, published by A. Whitman (1949).

Mariko Turk

Florida is home to the Baldwin Library of Historical Children's Literature.

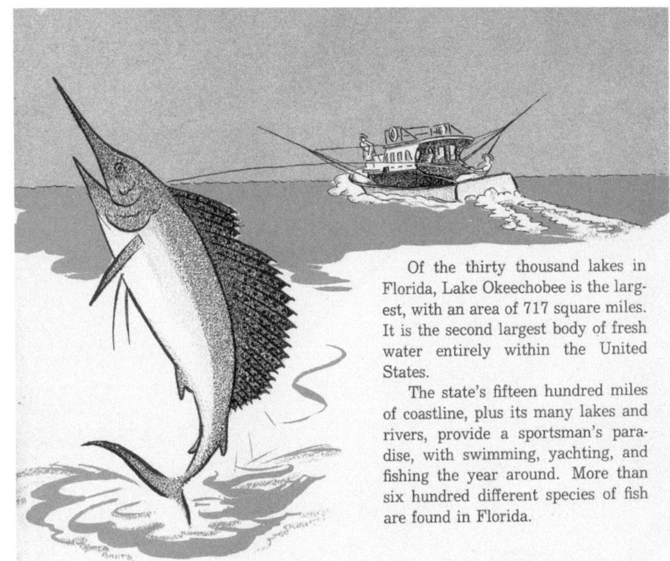

Of the thirty thousand lakes in Florida, Lake Okeechobee is the largest, with an area of 717 square miles. It is the second largest body of fresh water entirely within the United States.
The state's fifteen hundred miles of coastline, plus its many lakes and rivers, provide a sportsman's paradise, with swimming, yachting, and fishing the year around. More than six hundred different species of fish are found in Florida.

is for Florida

The Baldwin Library contains many books that showcase this subtropical state throughout the ages. Whether exploring the orange groves in winter, the orchids in the Everglades, or the ostrich farms in St. Augustine, books in the Baldwin depict Florida as a land rich in beauty, adventure, history, and nature.

Bernadine Bailey and Kurt Weise's *Picture Book of Florida* (1949) captures a variety of Florida's charms, including the romance of the Suwannee River, the bustling beaches of Miami, and the spectacular circus in Sarasota. The book begins with Juan Ponce de Leon's 1513 arrival in what is now St. Augustine, where he was so struck by the natural beauty of the landscape that he named it "La Florida" ("Place of Flowers"). The book ends with the industrialization of Florida's landscape in the early twentieth century, as the state became an important part of the nation's phosphate industry.

▲ ***Picture Book of Florida,*** by Bernadine Bailey, illustrated by, Kurt Wiese, published by A. Whitman (1949).

▼ ***Florida Sea Shells,*** by Bertha Aldrich, published by Houghton Mifflin (1978).

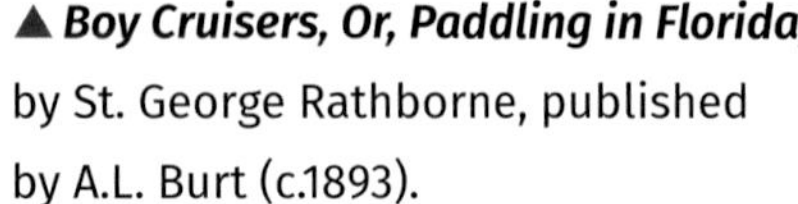

▲ ***Boy Cruisers, Or, Paddling in Florida,***
by St. George Rathborne, published
by A.L. Burt (c.1893).

"THERE! THERE!" SCREAMED GRACE. "THERE'S AN ALLIGATOR!"—*Page* 76.
The Outdoor Girls in Florida.

▲ ***Outdoor Girls in Florida,***
by Laura Lee Hope, published
by Grosset and Dunlap (1913).

Even amidst Florida's increasing industrialization, many Baldwin books highlight the persistent beauty of the state's natural wonders. Bertha Aldrich and Ethel Snyder's *Florida Sea Shells* (1936), for example, explores the diverse ocean "treasures" that appear on Florida's shores. In addition to detailing the features and families of mussels, whelks, sea snails, clams, conches, cowries, and cockles, the book's dreamy, descriptive prose paints shell collecting on Florida beaches as an enchantingly peaceful pastime.

Florida also serves as the landscape for many fictional yarns. Within the Baldwin's robust collection of late nineteenth and early twentieth-century series and adventure books are many that take place in the lively (and often perilous) setting of an imagined Florida. Some examples include St. George Rathborne's *The Boy Cruisers, or, Paddling in Florida* (1893), Laura Lee Hope's *The Outdoor Girls in Florida,* or, *Wintering in the Sunny South* (1913), and W. L. Alden's *The Loss of Swansea: A Story of the*

▲ ***Robert and Harold, or, the Young Marooners,*** by F. R. Goulding, illustrated by Harrison Weir, published by G. Routledge & Co. (1856).

▲ ***Loss of the Swansea,*** by W. L. Alden, illustrated by F.O. Small, published by D. Lothrop & Company (c.1889).

Florida Coast (1889). In many of these books, the Floridian landscape serves as a colorful, if not entirely nuanced, setting for adventure.

Some Florida fiction, however, pairs exciting stories with historical and environmental insight. Author and illustrator Lois Lenski won a Newbery Award for *Strawberry Girl* (1945), which details the daily joys and hardships of early twentieth-century life on the Florida "frontier," as families transitioned from traditional to modern ways of farming. Lenski travelled throughout central Florida—photographing, sketching, and documenting the culture and landscape—in preparation to write the book. Environmentalist, activist, and journalist Marjory Stoneman Douglas, whose writings about the Everglades were influential to its preservation, wrote a children's novel with a similar message of conservationism. *Alligator Crossing* (1959) tells the story of a boy who comes of age during a vivid journey through the Everglades, becoming aware of both himself and the ecosystem.

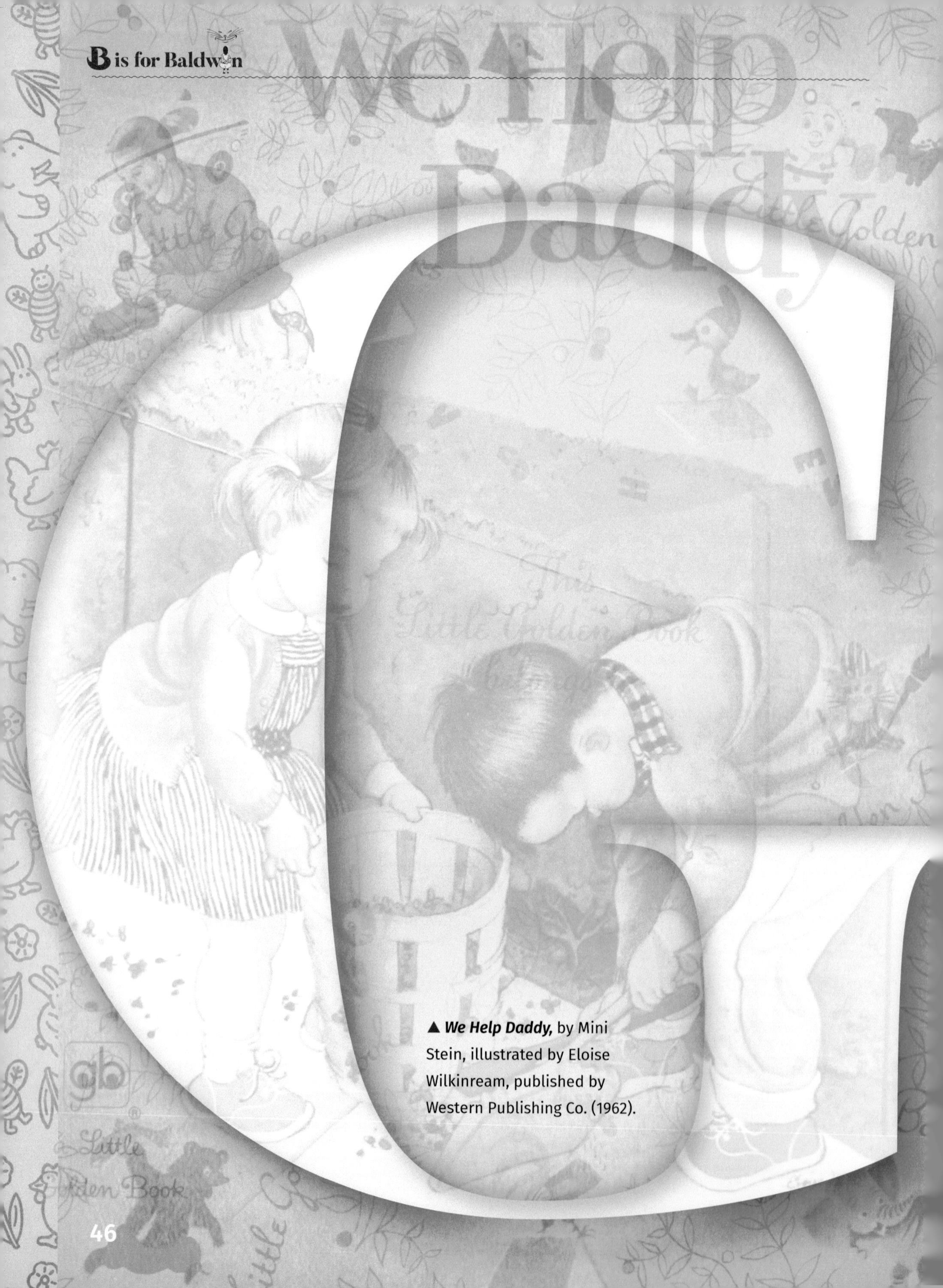

▲ ***We Help Daddy,*** by Mini Stein, illustrated by Eloise Wilkinream, published by Western Publishing Co. (1962).

G is for Golden Books

▲ ***The Poky Little Puppy,*** by Janette Sebring Lowrey, illustrated by Gustaf Tenggren, published by Simon & Schuster (1942).

Julie A. S. Cassidy

Hidden in the temperature controlled, moveable stacks of the Baldwin are over 600 Little Golden Books (LGBs) neatly lined up and alphabetized by title.

They are easy to identify with their signature gold-foil spine, but they are also easily overlooked since they are the ordinary stuff of childhood and have not been lauded with awards. Yet, 80 years after first being published, the LGBs continue to be a normalized and nostalgic part of growing up in America.

When the first fourteen LGBs were produced in 1942, the buying public marveled at their clever story lines and their inexpensive pricing. The first ten books included *The Pokey Little Puppy* among others that are now considered classics of children's literature. Since then, over 1,300 various LGB titles have been published. One might think that owning over 600 titles when more than 1300 titles are available is not a terribly interesting feat, but the Baldwin houses one of the largest, public collections of LGBs. Only two other collections are larger: the publishing house's own collection and that of a private collector in California who has direct ties to the publishing house.

The greatest strength of the Baldwin's LGB collection is that it so easily encapsulates the crossroads at which children's reading interests meet the dominant discourse of the United States. For one, the collection includes several pre-1945 LGBs that still have their dust jackets. These books provided a ready-made space throughout World War II for one of the main characters to address the child reader directly about the importance of buying and collecting U. S. War Savings Stamps. For another, the collection contains a variety of pop culture characters ranging from Donny and Marie Osmond (music) to Big Bird (*Sesame Street*), Cinderella (Disney), Huckleberry Hound (Hanna-Barbera), and Lassie (film and TV).

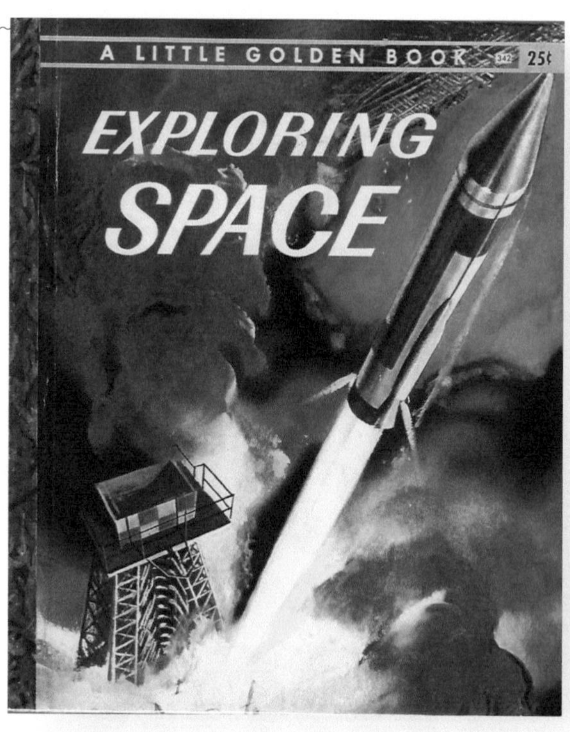

▲ ***Exploring Space,*** by Rose Wyler, illustrated by Tibor Gergely, published by Golden Press (1958).

▼ ***Fun With Decals,*** by Elsa Ruth Nast, illustrated by Corinne Malvern, published by Simon and Schuster (1952).

Moreover, one will find LGBs whose original artwork was changed for current republication. The 1959 version of *Cars and Trucks* includes children who are playing cowboys and Indians and a dad who is reading the paper outside while mom is washing dishes inside with a baby. In the new 1970s version, a little boy and a little girl play baseball, while dad takes care of the baby inside, and mom sits outside reading. First published in 1962, the cover of *We Help Daddy* features a father smoking a pipe while he clips the hedges with his two children nearby; the 70s publication removed the pipe. The 1948 cover of Ruth and Harold Shane's *The New Baby* shows an infant sleeping on their stomach; the 1975 version features a baby on their back. These are only a handful of the many changes and deletions that the Baldwin collection holds.

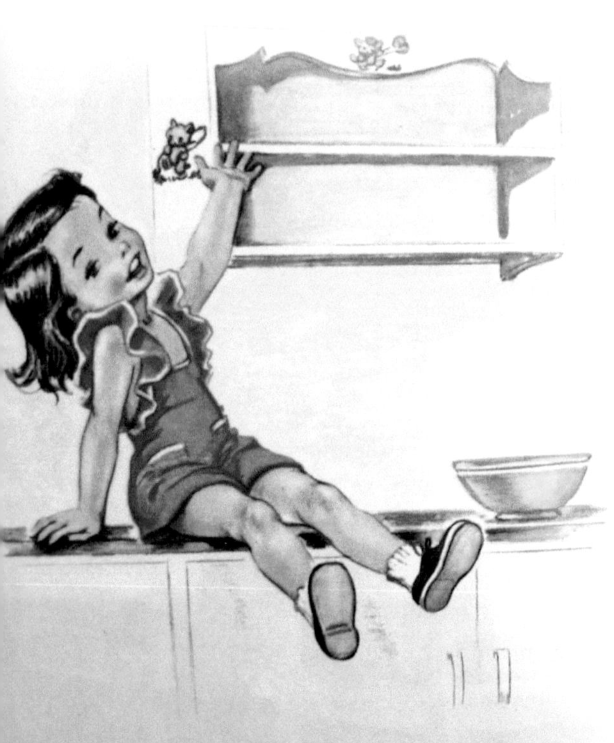

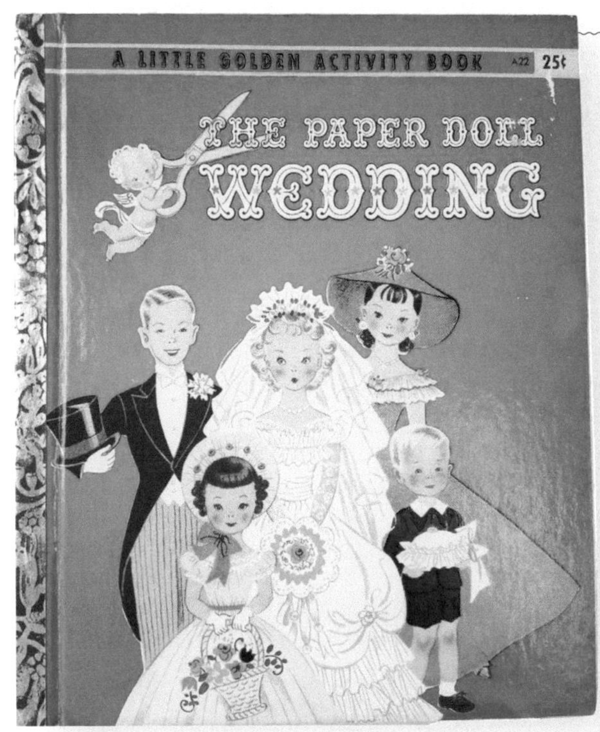

Does the LGB collection in the Baldwin contain additional treasures? Absolutely. Some of the books are unlikely to be republished, such as *Exploring Space* (1958) by Rose Wyler since it takes place long before the first moon landing in 1969, and the animals featured—like space mutt Laika—died in orbit. Other treasures include Little Golden Activity Books like *Fun With Decals* (1952), *The Paper Doll Wedding* (1954), and *Cowboy Stamps* (1957). All of these books, plus many more not mentioned here, make up a wonderful slice of American history that cannot be easily found elsewhere. ⩛

▲ ***The Paper Doll Wedding,*** by Hilda Miloche, published by Simon and Schuster (1954).

▼ ***Cowboy Stamps,*** by John Lyle Shimek, published by Simon and Schuster (1957).

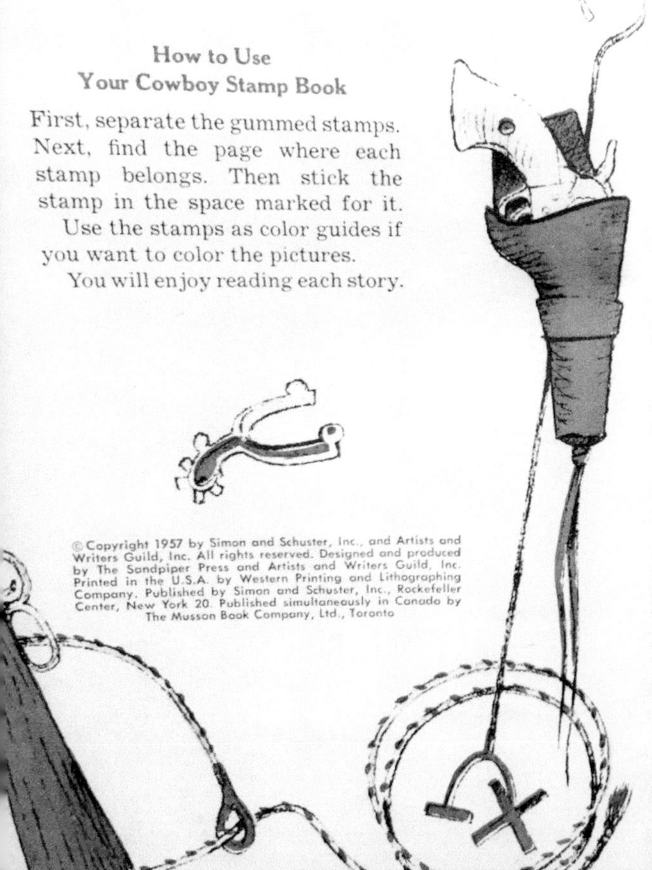

COLUMBIA UNIVERSITY

How to Use
Your Cowboy Stamp Book

First, separate the gummed stamps. Next, find the page where each stamp belongs. Then stick the stamp in the space marked for it.

Use the stamps as color guides if you want to color the pictures.

You will enjoy reading each story.

© Copyright 1957 by Simon and Schuster, Inc., and Artists and Writers Guild, Inc. All rights reserved. Designed and produced by The Sandpiper Press and Artists and Writers Guild, Inc. Printed in the U.S.A. by Western Printing and Lithographing Company. Published by Simon and Schuster, Inc., Rockefeller Center, New York 20. Published simultaneously in Canada by The Musson Book Company, Ltd., Toronto

Cowboy

A cowboy's job is to take care of the cows on a ranch. He sees that they have grass to eat and water to drink and keeps them from getting mixed up with other people's cows. He has to watch them all the time.

THE FIRST SINGING OF THE "MARSEILLAISE."

▲ ***Living Pages from Many Ages,*** by Mary Hield, published by Cassell, Petter, Galpin & Co. (1879).

Suzan Alteri

Learning from other people's lives is a concept older than literature itself, so it's no surprise that books about the celebrated, the great, and the famous men who exemplified the very idea of a role model, were some of the most popular literature printed for children.

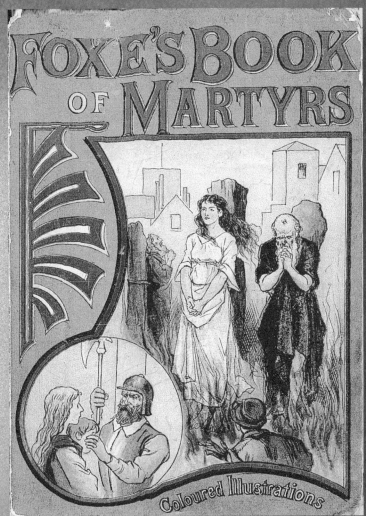

is for Historical Biographies

▲ ***Book of Martyrs,*** by John Foxe, published Frederick Warne and Co. (1887).

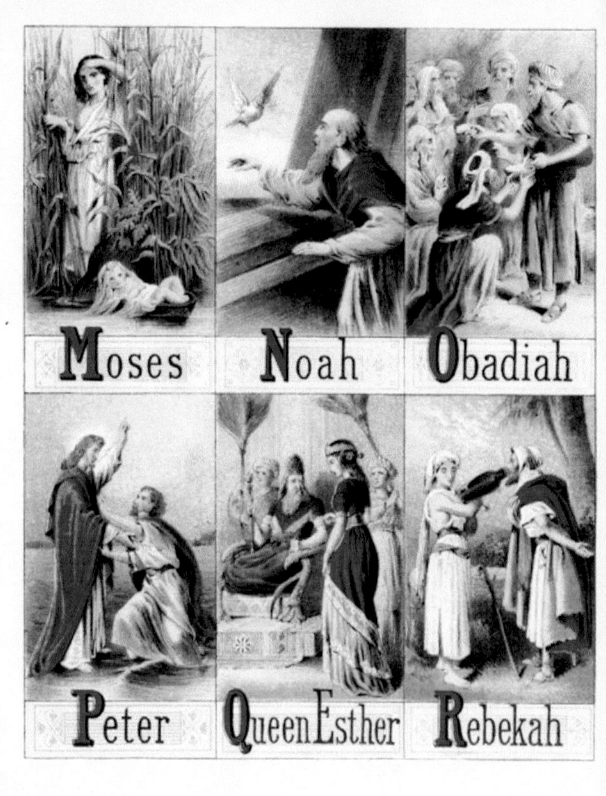

▲ ***Scripture Picture Alphabet,*** published by Thomas Nelson & Sons (c.1880).

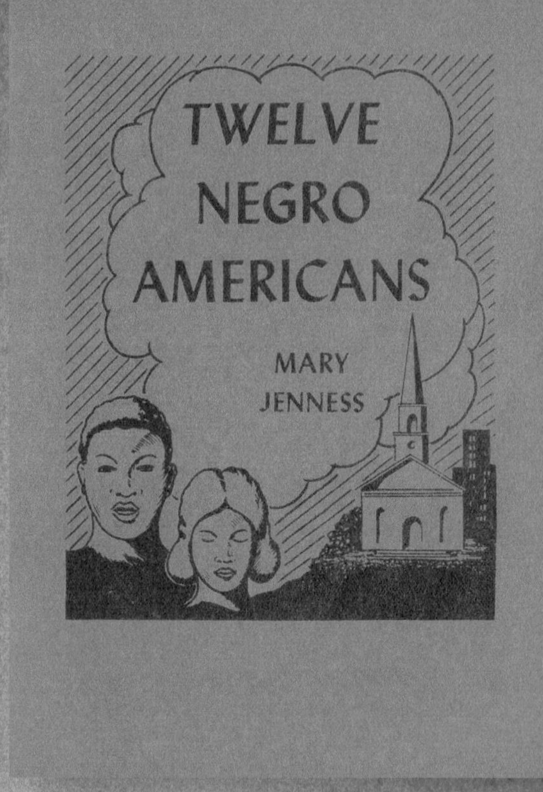

▲ ***Twelve Negro Americans,*** by Mary Jenness, published by Friendship Press, Inc. (1936).

The Baldwin Library has over 5,000 texts about the lives of both the living and the dead, real and imaginary, and even biographies of pincushions and mice. All these books add up to a historical pastiche of learning by example, and, in some, avoiding the pitfalls of those who came before you.

We can only imagine what children thought when reading works like James Janaway's *A Token for Children* (1671), which chronicled the lives and "happy deaths" of 13, children or the *Boy Princes*, stories of 20 royal boys doomed to fill an untimely grave. But what is certain is that kids' appetite or, at the very least, their parents' appetite, for prodigious and virtuous examples of young men and to a lesser degree, women, has been insatiable and steady since the mid-eighteenth century. Thankfully, the 'happy' deaths of small children soon gave way to more palatable books about courageous Christian reformers, as in *Brave Boys who have Become Illustrious Men of Our Time* (1884), and the heroic Esther, which an anonymous author summed up to readers in *Scripture*

Female Portraits (1820) "Oh! May her virtues all in you be seen/And be an Esther, tho' you're not a queen." Even the youngest of readers can't dismiss such nuggets of didactic gold.

Not all biographies focused on the virtuous and saintly among us. Henry St. Clair's *United States Criminal Calendar, or, an Awful Warning to the Youth of America* (1833) recounted the dealings of highway robbers and horrendous murderers in such full detail one wonders if he didn't give some enterprising youths a taste for the criminal. And if children couldn't find inspiration among the real lives of great men and women, they could always read the life stories of animals, as in the extraordinarily popular *Life and Perambulations of a Mouse* or the decidedly less popular *Blinky: the Story of a Ringtail* (1936). Animals not to your taste? Try Isaac Taylor's *Biography of a Brown Loaf* (1829), which details the, 'life', of bread from seedling to belly.

As the 20th century dawned, biographies for the young started to incorporate more modern ideas of self-awareness and more varied people, such as women and people of color. Helen Josephine Ferris interviewed real women in their careers for *Girls Who Did* (1927). Ferris even concluded her work with a chapter entitled "You," a rather interesting addition that wanted readers to ask themselves, "What about Me?" Mary Jenness' *Twelve Negro Americans* (1936), published by the National Council of Churches to promote racial diversity and race relations, was summed up in the *American Journal of Sociology* as ". . . the struggles and achievements of fourteen Negroes who, while they are not nationally known, have carved out niches for themselves in their particular spheres" (vol. 42, 6).

Perusing such a wide array of biographies, one realizes that not much has changed in the genre—at least in children's books. Sure, we've dialed down the moralizing tenor of many of these works, but biographies are still in the business of teaching by example. And while we may never reach the royal heights of Esther or be immortalized for our social reforms, the authors—both new and old—certainly want us to try.

▶ ***Heroes and Heroines,*** by Eleanor and Herbert Farjean, illustrated by Rosalind Thornycroft, published by E. P. Dutton & Co., Inc. (c.1940).

E,e.

▼ ***An ABC for Baby Patriots,*** by Mary Ames, published by Dean & Son (1899).

is for Imperialism

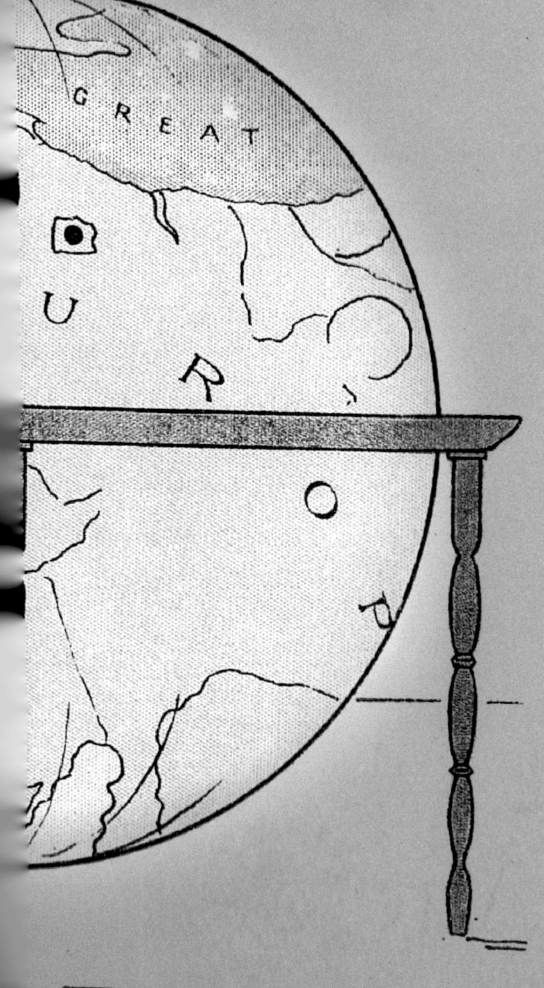

Megan Norcia

With what trembling fingers and racing hearts must small readers have turned the pages of these books, upon which they left their names, their marginalia, and dog-eared edges.

For them, participation in the work of empire promised a journey beyond the glimmering horizon, deep into Joseph Conrad's "blank spaces" on the map. In the novels and geographies in the Baldwin Library, we can trace their footsteps.

Imperialism takes many forms in the "blood and thunder" adventure novels by R.M. Ballantyne, W.H.G. Kingston, the G.A. Henty, and lesser-known Emilia Marryat, L.T. Meade, and Bessie Marchant. From planting a flag or signing a treaty, to shipping ivory, harvesting tea, panning for gold beneath burning suns, to slipping through a crowded souk, preaching to converts beneath palm-fringed skies, firing a musket on a sandy plain, stalking tigers through the jungle, or rounding the Horn in tumultuous seas—the novels offer multiple modes of filling in those blank spaces. Readers could defend the stockade with Masterman Ready; save a comely Indigenous princess and convert pirates to Christianity while colonizing *The Coral Island*; they could cook giant land crabs in *Four on an Island*. These books insert child protagonists and readers into the imperial project, yoking their personal ambitions to an urgent sense of imperial duty and setting up an often adversarial relationship to Indigenous peoples who are either aggressors to be conquered or victims to be saved.

A lesser-known body of imperial texts well represented in the Baldwin are geography primers. Alongside popular geographers like Abbé Gaultier and Samuel Goodrich are more obscure women writers, evangelists Mary Martha Sherwood and Favell Lee Mortimer, and those who combined the novel and geographic genres (Priscilla Wakefield, Barbara Hofland) or travelogues (Annie Keary). Harriet Beecher Stowe's geography appears in the collection (with a revision by an English lady which softens some remarks about US supremacy). These authors employ various methods to depict imperialism as creating an orderly garden out of a chaotic wilderness. The anonymous *Geography in Easy Dialogues* offers a conversational approach, and Annie Wright Marston's *Children of India* instructs children to join local missionary efforts and support those abroad, publicized in Henriette McDougall's *Letters from Sarawak.*

▶ ***Introduction to the Manual of Geography,*** by James Monteith, published by A.S. Barnes and Company (1871).

Geography and History Selected By a Lady for the Use of her Own Children uses the guise of science to advance an imperial agenda, privileging Christian nations who embrace the duty of converting the colonized. The important partnership between religion and imperialism was fostered by the Society for the Promotion of Christian Knowledge, and the Religious Tract Society, firms which published conversion narratives such as Mary Martha Sherwood's *Little Henry and his Bearer*. Books in the Baldwin often contain Sunday school prize labels or "favorite aunt" dedications adding an extra layer of depth and interaction.

The size and complexity of the Baldwin Library is tremendously exciting. While some works are straightforward, others subtly undermine imperialism; for example, Mary Ames' picture book *An ABC for Baby Patriots* initially seems pro-imperial, but closer analysis reveals that it satirizes imperial greed and questions imperial politics. However sophisticated the text or the reader, the novels, geographies, and hybrids collected in the Baldwin cultivated an imperial worldview in child readers who saw themselves poised on the edge of a great destiny, ready to take up the "white man's burden" in far-flung locales. The Library reveals the places where this ambition is crossed by competing concerns about gender, religious duty, scientific interests, commercial interests, or military aims.

▲ ***Shadows on the Screen,*** George Cupples, published by T. Nelson and Sons (1883).

▶ ***Our Parlour Panorama,*** by George Cupples, published by T. Nelson and Sons (1882).

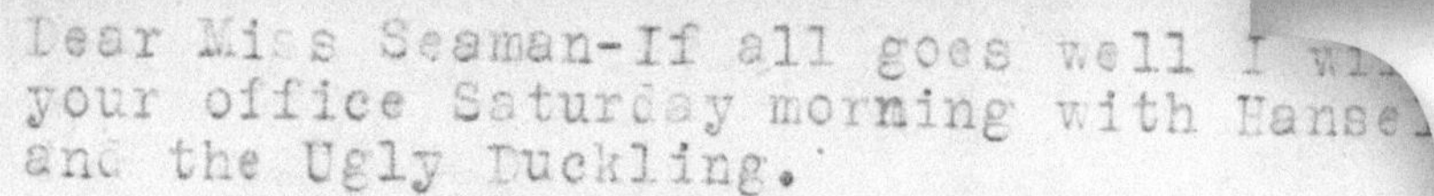

Dear Miss Seaman-If all goes well I wi
your office Saturday morning with Hanse
and the Ugly Duckling.

ELMER STANLEY HADER
RIVER ROAD
NYACK, NEW YORK

▲▶ ***Louise Seaman Bechtel Papers.***
Baldwin Library of Historical
Children's Literature.
University of Florida.

JoAnn Conrad

In 1919, Louise Seaman (later Bechtel) was hired by the Macmillan Publishing Company to head its new children's book department, the first of its kind.

is for Juvenile Editors

Dearest Louise,
In times like these,
Though bones may break
And rivers frese,
Remember still
In all your woe
Your loving friends
Who miss you soe,
And trust this little box of bigni
Will do its best to ease your mis'ri!

MB RF

▲ ***Louise Seaman Bechtel Papers.*** Baldwin Library of Historical Children's Literature. University of Florida.

Seaman's appointment signaled the growing market in children's books, but, more importantly, the introduction of an entirely new kind of children's book—highly illustrated and marketed to the lower end of the market. She also invented novel approaches to marketing, using serialized collections and illustrated catalogs. Seaman's entry into the new field of children's book publishing was followed by a number of women who would head other children's book divisions—May Massee at Doubleday, Alice Dagliesh at Scribner, Lucille Ogle with the Little Golden Books and others. These early women editors developed and maintained personal relationships both with their authors and illustrators and each other. They were

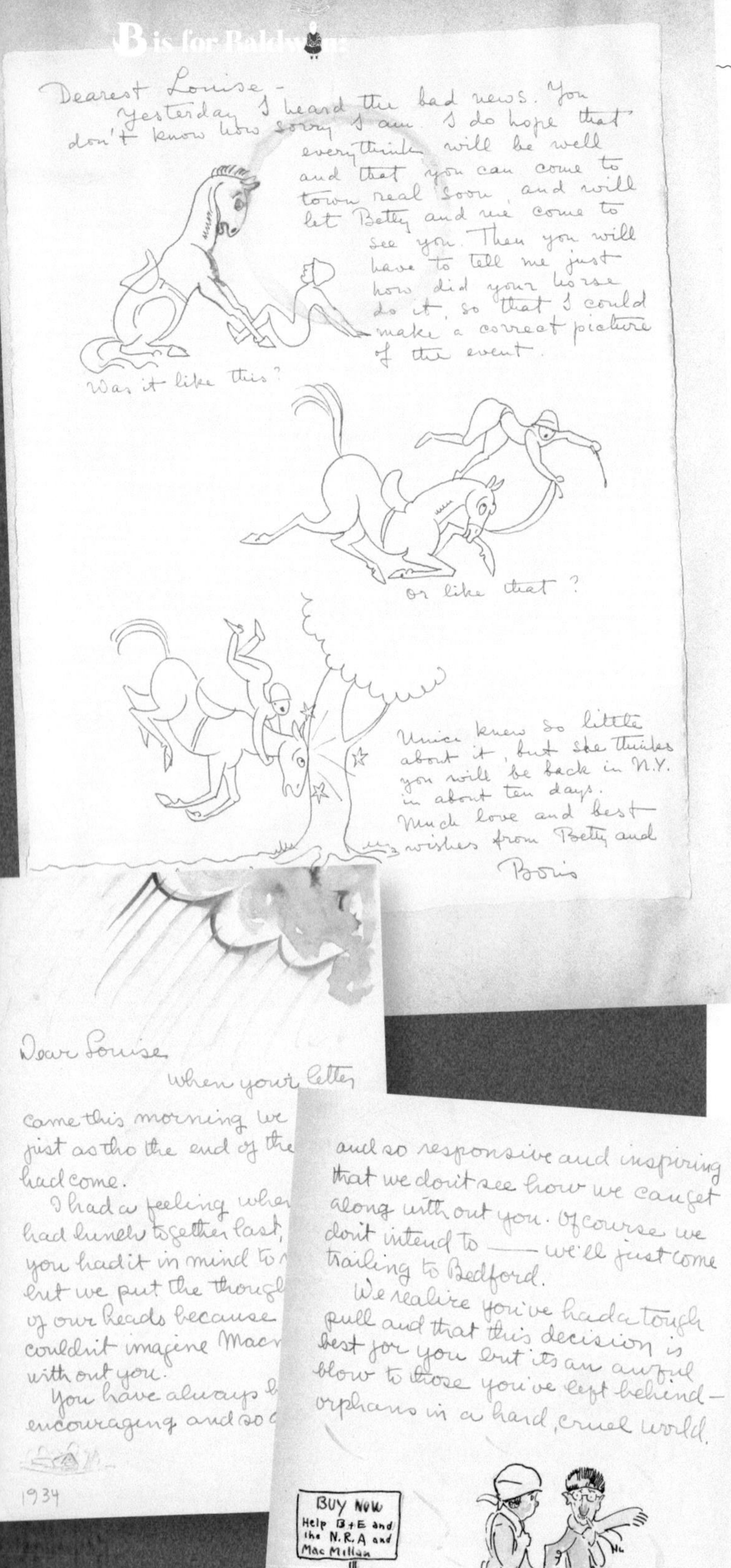

Dearest Louise -
Yesterday I heard the bad news. You don't know how sorry I am. I do hope that everything will be well and that you can come to town real soon and will let Betty and me come to see you. Then you will have to tell me just how did your horse do it, so that I could make a correct picture of the event.

Was it like this?

Or like that?

Unice knew so little about it, but she thinks you will be back in N.Y. in about ten days.
Much love and best wishes from Betty and
Boris

Dear Louise,
When your letter came this morning we ... just as tho the end of the ... had come.
I had a feeling whe... had lunch together last, you had it in mind to ... but we put the thoug... of our heads because ... couldn't imagine Mac... without you.
You have always b... encouraging and so ...

1934

and so responsive and inspiring that we don't see how we can get along without you. Of course we don't intend to —— we'll just come trailing to Bedford.
We realize you've had a tough pull and that this decision is best for you but its an awful blow to those you've left behind — orphans in a hard, cruel world.

actively engaged in the book publishing process from beginning to end, and it is no stretch to say that the nature of the final products—the children's books produced at least until the WW II—is the result, at least in part, of these personal bonds. Evidence of these long-lasting personal relationships are attested to in the many letters and correspondences between these women editors and their illustrators and authors. The Louise Seaman Bechtel Archive and Manuscript Collection, housed at the Baldwin Library, contains many such personal letters to Seaman that shine a particular light not only on lives, but also on aspects of a children's publishing world that has long since disappeared.

Part of Seaman's vision was to create highly illustrated, cheap-to-produce, pocket-sized books which working-class families could afford, and in order to keep costs down, she relied on previous relationships while recruiting relatively unknown new talent. Some of her authors, such as Elizabeth Coatsworth, were classmates from Vassar. For illustrators, Seaman often turned to fresh unknowns or newly arrived immigrant authors. To launch what would become the "Happy Hour Book" series, Seaman held a contest—new illustrations for Hans Christian Andersen's *The Ugly Duckling*. Elmer and Berta Hader, who had illustrated children's material for women's magazines but never children's books, were

◀ ***Louise Seaman Bechtel Papers.*** **Baldwin Library of Historical Children's Literature. University of Florida.**

Seaman's first choice, and thus began a relationship between Seaman, the Haders, and Macmillan that would last for decades. An illustrated letter from the Haders to Seaman commemorates the delivery of their final illustrations for that first book.

The Haders would go on to illustrate more than 70 books for Macmillan, as well as books for Doubleday, Knopf, Whitman, and other publishers well into the 1960s. Seaman's tenure at Macmillan, however, was abruptly terminated in 1934, as did her professional correspondence with the Haders (their subsequent correspondences with Bechtel's successor at Macmillan, Doris Patee, are housed at the University of Oregon). Their personal letters, all illustrated, continued, however, as seen in this 1951 thank-you note after a Bechtel Rose party.

In 1934, Seaman, now Bechtel, had a riding accident and was hospitalized. Illustrators and authors sent their condolences and did their best to visualize the series of events. The injuries were serious, however, and coincided with Bechtel's resignation from Macmillan. Because Seaman had developed such personal relationships with so many authors and illustrators, their dismay at her precipitous departure is expressed in their letters. Some, however, like Rachel Field, aware of Seaman's deteriorating relationship with the new head of Macmillan, Mr. Brett, Jr., were skeptical of the official reason for her departure. In her letter to Brett (in the appendix to Seaman's unpublished (digitized) autobiography), Field states: "If it were merely a long leave of absence, anything but a final resignation, there might be a chance of my going on with the same old enthusiasm. As it is, I feel, as so many others do, that a very real force has gone out of literature for children." Bechtel collated the cards and letters, often with original artwork into a scrapbook that is housed in the Baldwin Library.

These letters provide a unique and personal insight into the life and person of Louise Seaman Bechtel—a "real force" in children's literature in America during a formative period.

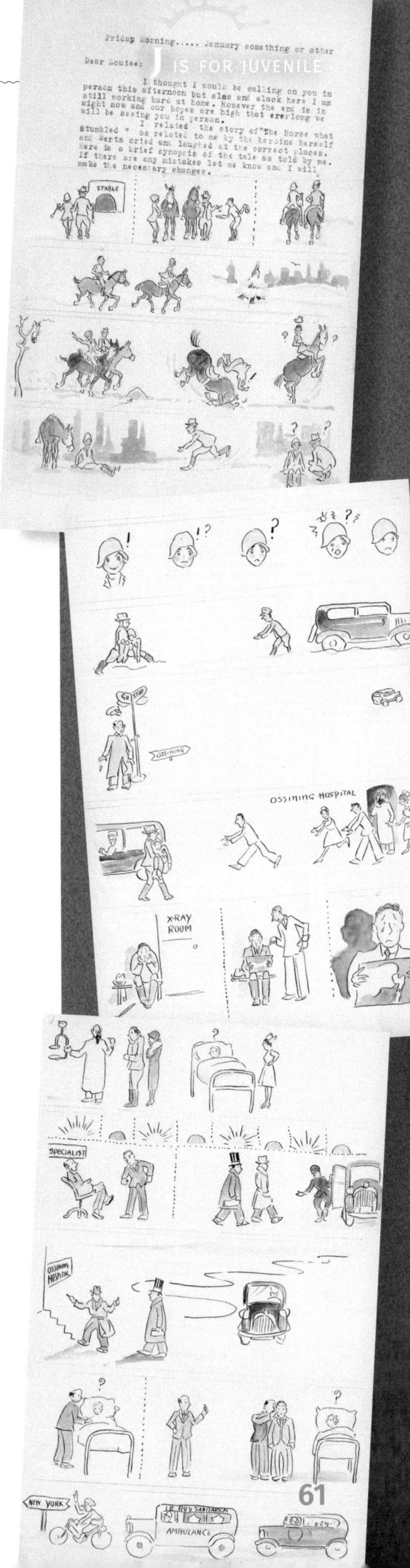

▶ ***Louise Seaman Bechtel Papers.*** Baldwin Library of Historical Children's Literature. University of Florida.

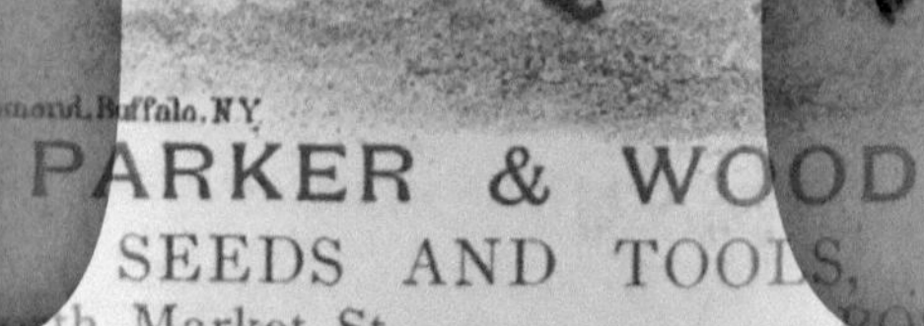

▲ Uncataloged scrapbooks obtained by Ruth Baldwin.

Noah Mullens

Heritage House porcelain, Precious Moment statues, Sheffield pewter baby steins, and decorative commemorative plates *(the ones nobody is allowed to use)*: **these are some of the kitschy, non-book treasures of the Baldwin Library.**

◀ Uncataloged postcard featuring a small girl among flowers, with a pull-tab that makes the card three-dimensional.

K is for Kitsch

The Oxford English Dictionary defines kitsch as "art characterized by worthless pretentiousness; to affect with sentimentality and vulgarity." This definition may be harsh, as some kitschy objects are homespun and made with love. In any case, kitsch has little aesthetic value according to the usual standards. You can put kitsch on display or hide in a closet; either way, there is something about it that makes it hard to give away. Kitsch is in the eye of the beholder; one person's precious art is another person's kitsch.

Kitschy items haunt the outskirts of the special collections. In the Baldwin, for instance, there is the main collection of books, and then there is the ancillary collection of odd and often kitschy objects. These are items that are donated or come with an estate. They are tangential to the collection, not usually catalogued, and often relegated to storage. Kitsch in the Baldwin and other special collections of children's literatures tend to be vestiges of adult nostalgia about childhood.

◀ Cover of an uncataloged scrapbook album for children, containing vivid advertisements and drawings ranging from the 1890s to the early 1900s.

Typically ignored by scholars, special collection kitsch is charming and interesting. As an example from the Baldwin, consider the 25+ small ceramic and plastic statues of children reading books. When Ruth Baldwin would go on collection trips, she would grab up inexpensive statues of children reading. Though these reflect the values of the collection, they are objects that are difficult to assess in relation to the books themselves. The statues do, however, inscribe scenes of reading in diverse ways. The Baldwin holds ceramics of Cabbage Patch Kids reading together in various pastel furniture pieces. There is also a plastic statue of Big Bird reading a blue book. In the case of some porcelain, like the 1998 Heritage House "My Mother's Love," the pages of the books that are usually hidden from a viewer are clearly illustrated with scribbles, cats, and a picture of a girl. There is also the rare toy that is an adaptation of a children's book, like the two toys of Pinocchio, both with moveable joints and long noses made from wood. Baldwin also collected block puzzles and other toys that encouraged play and education.

Also in the Baldwin are some kitschy craft pieces. Most scholars don't bestow handcrafted work to the collections they visit, but Gillian Avery did, making embroidered pieces for both the Baldwin and the American Antiquarian Society. Avery, a British children's novelist and children's literature scholar, worked closely with Baldwin while researching her book, *Behold the Child: American Children and their Books 1621-1922* (1995). When Baldwin passed away in 1990, Avery embroidered a memorial piece that included characters from books found in Baldwin's sampler, *100 Nineteenth Century Rhyming Alphabets in English* (1972), such as the ungroomed boy from *The English Struwwelpeter*.

Or consider the enigmatic scrapbook of vivid advertisements and drawings ranging from the 1890s to the early 1900s. Whoever produced this album cut out and pasted images in a deliberate fashion, overlapping common-

▲ **Embroidered memorial made by Dr. Gillian Avery, children's book author and scholar.**

alities (such as entire pages dedicated to illustrations of newborns) or highlighting the comical (such as preserving an ad where a woman's body is made out of a corn cob). From Ruth Baldwin's office is another scrapbook, whose pages are filled with vintage cut-outs organized thematically. One page spotlights cats, where an image of a cat beside a barrel is circled by smaller cat faces. In the middle of the scrapbook we find a postcard featuring a small girl among flowers, with a pull-tab that makes the card three-dimensional.

The Love Bank, however, is a specimen of exemplary kitsch. It is a plastic box in vivid blue and green, whose top is adorned by two child figurines waiting to kiss every time a coin is placed in the slot. These items invite users, ranging from kids to scholars, to engage with them. We wonder how the Love Bank works—does dropping in a coin actually move the figures together?—and we wonder why the act of saving is equated with a (shy?) kiss. Maybe, then, scholars should search through these ancillary collections and interact with them to glean what they can. One thing for sure is that these items are not going away any time soon.

▲ Assorted figurines of children reading, which Ruth Baldwin collected.

▶ The Love Bank made by Yap in the mid-twentieth century.
Photo credit: Noah Mullens

▲ Photograph of the stacks of the Baldwin Library, where the books are shelved by size.

Spencer Chalifour

is for Little Books for Little Hands

▲ ***Cabinet of Lilliput,*** published by J. Harris (1802).

▲ ***David Copperfield,*** by Dickens, retold by Eleanor Packer, published by Whitman Publishing Company (1934).

Imagine the most thrilling adventure yarns, the most hilarious comedies, and literature's most esteemed classics shrunk down to fit in the palm of your hand. Such is the appeal of the paradoxically titled Big Little Books.

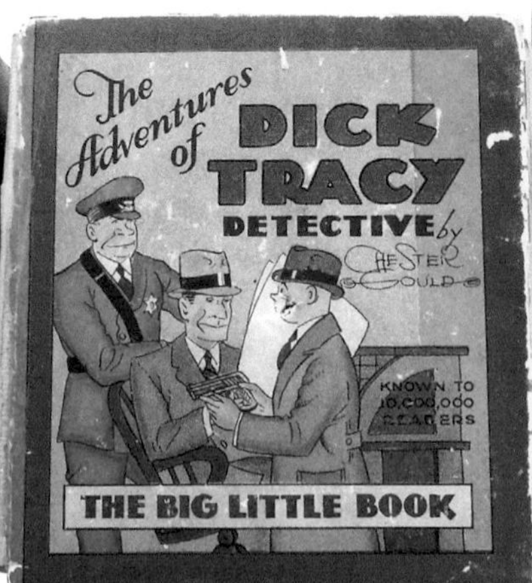

▲ ***The Green Hornet Strikes,*** by Fran Striker, illustrated by Robert R. Weisman, published by Whitman Publishing Co. (1940).

▲ ***The Adventures of Dick Tracy Dectective,*** by Chester Gould, published by Whitman Publishing Co. (1932).

▲ ***The Return of Tarzan,*** by Edgar Rice Burroughs, published by Whitman Publishing Co. (1936).

From the 1930s to the 1960s, these thick yet miniscule illustrated books achieved immense popularity among young readers.

The name "Big Little Books" specifically refers to the series published by Whitman Publishing, located in Racine, Wisconsin, though the name grew to encompass books with similar dimensions from other publishers. Whitman itself also published these books under the title "Better Little Books" starting in 1938.

Small books designed for a young audience did not originate with this series, however. During the latter half of the 19th century, miniature books were popular with readers of all ages. Some illustrated miniatures created for children provided instruction to young readers in a variety of subjects, from history to biology to morality. Prayer books and poetry collections for children were also popular in miniature form. The Baldwin is home to several of these books, including *My Pet Box of Books,* published by Leavitt & Allen in 1855, which includes a book-shaped box that holds 11 even smaller tomes with titles like "Stories of Dogs" and "Child's Book of Natural History."

Whitman's Big Little Books had a stronger focus on entertainment than education, and this series adapted both visual media, like comic strips and movies, and non-visual media, like pulp fiction stories and radio shows, as opposed to telling wholly original stories. The first Big Little Book was published in December

◀ ***Tiny Nonsense Stories,*** created by Dorothy Kunhardt, illustrated by Garth Williams, published by Simon & Schuster (1948).

1932, predating what many historians consider the first true comic book, *Famous Funnies #1* (cover-dated July 1934), by over a year. This first volume, *The Adventure of Dick Tracy*, adapts a series of comic strips featuring Chester Gould's titular detective into an illustrated prose story, thereby achieving what early comic books would later accomplish—collecting multiple comic strips into a single anthology that could be sold to children for 10¢.

Three main approaches to storytelling emerge when examining the Baldwin's collection of Big Little Books. The first, and by far most popular, approach uses only prose text on one page with an illustration on the opposing page. However, other books include an illustration on each page, with the story's text beneath this picture, while others simply reprint comic strips by enlarging each panel so it takes up an entire page. Despite their differences, all three approaches represent sequential art, or storytelling that uses one image after another, usually accompanied with text, to tell a story. Big Little Books adapted from comic strips would obviously include this approach, but others adapted entirely different types of media to a sequential form, including the Tarzan novels of Edgar Rice Burroughs and the Green Hornet radio drama. Film adaptations were themselves adapted into Big Little Books, including MGM's *David Copperfield* from 1935, whose Big Little Book adaptation includes stills from the film instead of illustrations as well as a cast list on the first page. By allowing readers to re-experience the film long after it had left theaters, these film adaptations also act as precursors to home video.

Though children's books with similar storytelling approaches and dimensions have been published sporadically since the 1960s, Big Little Books are now relegated to mostly being objects of nostalgia. However, the Baldwin's collection of these books remains a fascinating testament to the visual culture of the 1930s that included the emergence of sound films, cartoons, and comic books, all of which received the Big Little Book treatment.

▲ ***My Pet Box of Books,*** published by Leavitt & Allen (185-).

▲ ***Histories, or, Tales of Past Times,*** by Charles Perrault, published by Philip Rose (1800).

John Cech

Who was Mother Goose, and why do we continue to celebrate her memory every time we teach a child a nursery rhyme, play patty-cake, or sing them a lullaby?

is for Mother Goose

▲ ***My First Picture Book,*** by Joseph Martin Kronheim, published by George Routledge & Sons (c.1871).

For each of us, she is the way that we tune ourselves to our cultures, its rhythms and rhymes, the beats of its daily activities, the sounds of its words, often silly or obscure, yet always necessary displays of word magic. Without her, our language would be impoverished, and every note would sound the same.

Mother Goose creates that place in childhood where we first hear language sung and thoroughly enjoyed. Many of those songs she sang that we still pass down

▶ ***The Baby's Opera a Book of Old Rhymes with New Dresses,*** by Walter Crane, published by McLoughlin Bros. (1878).

to our children make little sense to us today, though at the time when they first appeared they were popular ditties, sung in the fields, on the road, around the hearths, and in the taverns of England and America. They were verses about political leaders, current events, occupations, ethnic and gender stereotypes—part of the busy world of oral culture that is constantly being recreated, even today, in our print and media-saturated society.

One version of Mother Goose story is that she was French and from the eighth century A.D. Her name was Bertha, and she was the mother of Charlemagne, the first of the Holy Roman Emperors. She is said to have been a vibrant woman, full of rhymes, songs, and stories, and, because of the larger size of one of her feet, she acquired the rather cruel nickname of "Queen Goosefoot." But the name, Mother Goose, first appeared in 1696 as the subtitle to one of the earliest collections of fairy tales, Charles Perrault's *Tales From My Mother Goose*. Almost a thousand years after Bertha, the Mother Goose name had made it into popular mythology to describe any older woman who told tales to children. There's even a picture of her—one of the first that we have—on the frontispiece of Perrault's book. In the "Archive for the History of Mother Goose," we also learn that another Bertha—from Norse and Germanic mythology—was not only the goddess of spinning but also the protector "of the souls of unborn children" and the soother of babies. She, too, is depicted as being surrounded by children, and she, too, has one larger foot, overdeveloped from her many hours pushing on the treadle of her spinning wheel.

▲ ***Mother Goose the Old Nursery Rhymes,*** by Arthur Rackham, published by William Heinemann (1913).

▲ ***Denslow's Mother Goose A.B.C. Book,*** by W. W. Denslow, published by G.W. Dillingham Co. (1904).

America lays some claim to Mother Goose as well. One version of this history has it that she was Elizabeth Goose, the highly talkative mother-in-law of the printer, Isaiah Thomas, in colonial Boston. He is said to have published a collection of her verses that she was forever reciting around the Thomas household. Yet a copy of that volume of those ditties has never been found, if it was ever printed at all. But whoever she was and is, and in whatever language she originally spoke and still speaks, we remember her because she has taught us all, in the words of the Welsh poet, Dylan Thomas, to "fall in love with words." And, quite simply, hers are the first lyrics to the song of life that we all learn to sing—by heart.

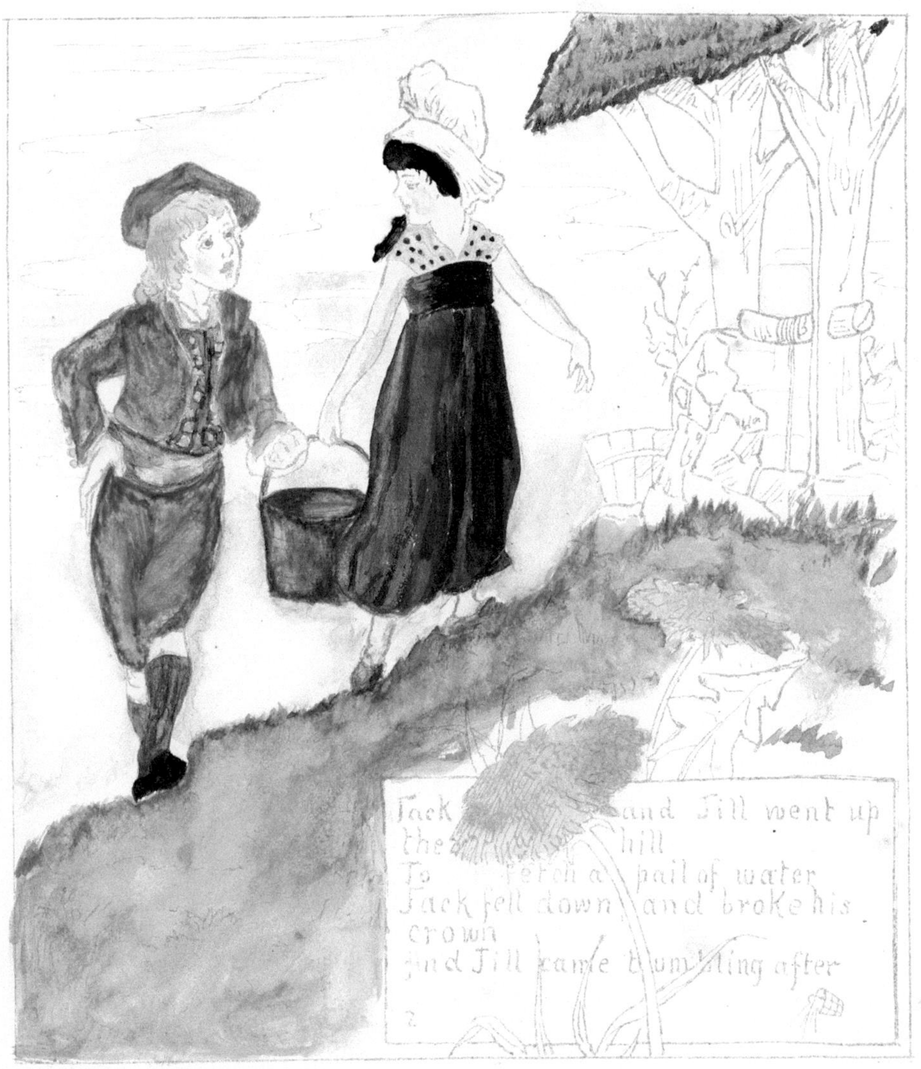

◀ ***Twenty Four Pictures from Mother Goose,*** **created and published by S.W. Tilton and Co. (c.1881).**

N

▲ ***Historical Marker.***
Photo credit: Tracy MacKay-Ratli

Laurie Taylor & Chelsea Dinsmore

is for NEH

"One cannot speak of history or culture apart from the humanities.

They not only record our lives; our lives are the very substance they are made of. Their subject is every man. We propose, therefore, a program for all our people, a program to meet a need no less serious than that for national defense. We speak, in truth, for what is being defended–our beliefs, our ideals, our highest achievements."[i]

Report of the Commission on the Humanities, leading to the creation of the National Endowment for the Humanities

▶ ***The New Robinson Crusoe an Instructive and Entertaining History for the Use of Children of Both Sexes,*** by Joachim Heinrich Campe, engravings by John Bewick, printed for John Stockdale (1789).

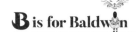

The Baldwin Digital Collection includes 7,849 titles with 1,259,075 pages.

▲ ***St. Nicholas,*** by Mary Mapes Dodge, published by Scribner (1874).

The history of the Baldwin Library of Historical Children's Literature is tied to the history of the National Endowment for the Humanities (NEH). The NEH began in 1965, as a federal investment in culture to complement investments in science. Glenn Seaborg, Nobel Laureate and then head of the Atomic Energy Commission, said of the creation of the NEH: "Science and technology are providing us with the means to travel swiftly. But what course do we take? This is the question that no computer can answer."[ii]

In 1977, the Baldwin Library was awarded one of the NEH's inaugural Challenge Grants. The grant proposal explained that the Baldwin would serve as a research collection for newly instituted humanistic programs at UF, and open the collection to the public for the first time. The history of the Baldwin and the NEH tells an ongoing tale of enduring efforts to open and expand public access while growing research and the humanities. The NEH provided substantial support for cataloging, microfilming, and digitization of holdings from the Baldwin with three major grants awarded in 2000, 2004, and 2007 for a total of $961,015.

As one of the largest open access digital collections of children's literature, the Baldwin's many pages have been viewed over 153 million times since the collection launched with the UF Digital Collections in 2006.

Importantly, the Baldwin Digital Collection pre-dates the UF Digital Collections, and helped lay the groundwork for creating digital collections at UF. When digitization of the Baldwin Library began, the extensive metadata, serial items, and curated collections exceeded the capacities of digital libraries. The needs of the Baldwin informed and shaped the technologies of the UF Digital Collections, which exceeds 16 million pages and 800,000 items. The Baldwin also contributed to other national programs, including multiple shows on *Recess*! which aired on National Public Radio from 2001-2008. Recognizing the importance of the Baldwin as a physical and digital destination, UF honored the Collection with a 2008 historical marker.

NEH funding supported the Baldwin's growth as a physical and digital collection. As the Baldwin has continually grown in importance, so too has the community for the Baldwin. Arguably the first Curator of the Baldwin serving fully in the digital age, Suzan Alteri, created the Baldwin Scholars Council, leveraging community and technology to foster the virtuous cycle of scholars, librarians, and the public. This continues the work of the Baldwin and the field of Children's Literature in and for the digital age, work made possible in part thanks to the NEH.

The founding document of the NEH begins with a quote by John Adams: "I must study politics and war that my sons may have liberty to study mathematics and philosophy. My sons ought to study mathematics and philosophy, geography, natural history and naval architecture, navigation, commerce, and agriculture, in order to give their children a right to study painting, poetry, music, architecture...." [iii]

[i] https://www.acls.org/wp-content/uploads/2021/11/Report-of-The-Commission-on-the-Humanities-1964.pdf.

[ii] Quote from "How the NEH-Got Its Start," https://www.neh.gov/about/history.

[iii] *Report of the Commision on the Humanities*, as listed above.

The Baldwin Library demonstrates the value and importance of the NEH and the study of children's literature and culture to the ideals and dreams in the founding of the United States.

NATIONAL ENDOWMENT FOR THE HUMANITIES

◀ ▶ ▲ ***Alice's Adventures in Wonderland,*** by Lewis Carroll, Illustrated by Mabel Lucie Attwell, published by Raphael Tuck & Sons (c.1910).

OUR YOUNG FOLKS

AN

ILLUSTRATED MAGAZINE

FOR

BOYS AND GIRLS.

EDITED BY

J. T. TROWBRIDGE, GAIL HAMILTON, AND LUCY LARCOM.

VOL. I.

BOSTON:

TICKNOR AND FIELDS,

124 TREMONT STREET.

1865.

312 *Our Dogs.*

...ate creature, white as snow, except one mouse-colored ear. H... ...ived with enthusiasm, and christened Giglio; the honors of his ...nd toilette were performed by Mademoiselles the young ladies ...knees, as if he had been in reality young Prince Giglio from fairy-l...

Of all beautiful shapes in dog form, never was there one more pe... this. His hair shone like spun glass, and his skin was as fine an... ...of a baby; his paws and ears were translucent like fine chi... ...and great, soft, tremulous dark eyes; his every movement see... graceful than the last. Whether running or leaping, or sitting i... attitudes on the parlor table among the ladies' embroidery-fram... great rose-colored bow under his throat, he was alike a thing of b... his beauty alone won all hearts to him.

When the papa first learned that a third dog had been introduc... household, his patience gave way. The thing was getting des... were being overrun with dogs; our house was no more a house ...nel; it ought to be called Cunopolis, — a city of dogs; he cou... would not have it so; but papa, like most other indulgent old ... was soon reconciled to the children's pets. In fact, Giglio was f... ...ing under the bed-clothes at the Professor's feet not two mornin... arrival, and the good gentleman descended with him in his arm... ...ast, talking to him in the most devoted manner: — "Poor little ... cold last night? and did he want to get into papa's bed? he ... down stairs, that he should"; — all which, addressed ...steel, and who could have jump... ...stair to the bottom like a feather, was sufficiently amusing.

Giglio's singular beauty and grace were his only merits; he ...

Kenneth Kidd

is for *Our Young Folks*

Everyone who was anyone on the nineteenth-century literary scene wrote for *Our Young Folks: An Illustrated Magazine for Boys and Girls*, **which debuted in 1865, before the Civil War had ended.**

A partial list of contributing talent includes Thomas Bailey Aldrich, James Russell Lowell, Harriet Beecher Stowe, Bayard Taylor, Lydia Maria Child, Louisa May Alcott, Henry Wadsworth Longfellow, and Elizabeth Stuart Phelps. Most of its contributors were American, and from New England in particular, but even our illustrious friend from across the pond, Charles Dickens, took a turn, with "The Magic Fishbone" in 1868. Edited by John Townsend Trowbridge, Gail Hamilton, and Lucy Larcom, *Our Young Folks* was the first of several important and long-running children's periodicals that appeared in the immediate postwar period. Others included

◀ ▲ ***Our Young Folks An Illustrated Magazine for Boys and Girls,*** edited by J.T. Trowbridge, Lucy Larcom, and Gail Hamilton, published by Ticknor and Fields (1865-1873).

HERE is an entertaining account, from a correspondent over the sea, of one of the ways by which Viennese children amuse themselves. We are sure our American young folks will like to hear his description of "A Half-hour on the Paradeplatz," and to see it illustrated.

A HALF-HOUR ON THE PARADEPLATZ.

"You do not know where the Paradeplatz is.— It is here in Vienna, Austria. It is an open park where the twenty thousand soldiers, who form the garrison of this city, are reviewed and exercised in arms. Some years ago they dug up all the trees that used to shade the ground, in order to make it suitable for this purpose. This rendered it also a favorable place for kite-flying. In the midday sun it is an uninviting common, but in the evening it is thronged with active players. And in the fall kite-flying is the sport that is uppermost in the minds of the young Viennese. Sometimes the children of a family bring with them their little wagon, containing their implements of play, and enjoy an hour's evening picnic, having the wagon for their rallying-point.

"A kite is called *Drachen* here. The name signifies a fabled flying serpent, a dragon. In Prussia they call it *Alf*, which means an air-spirit, an elfin. In France they name it *Cerf volant*, or flying deer; and we give it the name of a bird, the kite or hawk.

"The young Austrians love to flaunt in the air the double-headed Austrian eagle, and black and yellow, their national colors. Also one sees on the kites the emblems of different orders, that is, classes of men who are honored by the Emperor with a particular badge. Here is the Kaiser (Emperor), wearing the emblem of an order on his breast. And because Franz Josef, the Kaiser, married a Bavarian princess, the colors of Bavaria, blue and white, are adopted by many of the children.

"In Europe it is the custom that many families live in the same large house; and so the children have not much freedom to romp and halloo at home. Therefore the open space and free air of the common are doubly dear to them. But the winter will soon be here, when they will have to stay in the house and be quiet, and the kites too must be laid by. Next fall the old skeleton of sticks will be clothed with new paper and new colors, and the kite will have another life.

"Here they gather the apples in September, and in October they press the grapes for wine; but November is cool enough for active exercise,— Young November is therefore a hunter boy, with hound and horn. Here is his statue in the Belvedere palace garden."

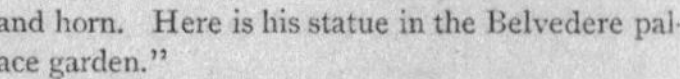

U. S. A. "Washington's Judgment" is not up to the mark.

ANSWER TO STRANGE STAIRWAYS.

First step, *do* (dough); second, *re* (ray); third, *mi* (me); fourth, *fa* (far); fifth, *sol* (soul); sixth, *la* (Lah); seventh, *si* (sea); eighth, *do* (dough). The stairways are the ascending and descending scales in music; the "folks of note" are the musical notes.

M. B. C. S.

Oliver Optic's Magazine, The Riverside Magazine for Young People and the even more prestigious *St. Nicholas. Youth's Companion* had paved the way for such periodicals, arriving much earlier in 1827 and eventually merging with *The American Boy*. The Baldwin boasts extensive runs of these magazines, many of them complete; it's one of the collection's strengths.

Designed for older children who could already read, but often enjoyed by the whole family, these periodicals were a crucial part of children's literature through the early twentieth century. They featured an impressive array of materials, including stories, essays, poems, and biographical sketches. Illustrations were likewise rich and diverse, although the written text took some priority. Many stories were serialized, such that readers would eagerly await the next issue's installment—no downloading and binge-watching the whole season! Trowbridge wrote some of the most popular serials for *Our Young Folks*, including *Jack Hazard and His Fortunes*. Not all the magazine's serials were so beloved, but many provide an intriguing glimpse into the period. *Farming for Boys*, for instance, tells the story of how a yeoman gentle-

▲ ▶ ***Our Young Folks An Illustrated Magazine for Boys and Girls***, edited by J.T. Trowbridge, Lucy Larcom, and Gail Hamilton, published by Ticknor and Fields (1865-1873).

80 *Round the Evening Lamp.* [January.

ILLUSTRATED REBUS.—No. 1.

H. M. T.

VON RAIL.

THERE was an old Dutchman, Von Rail,
Who had an ambition to sail,
So he put out to sea,
In a fit of high glee,
That hilarious old person, Von Rail.

450 *Farming for Boys.* [July,

FARMING FOR BOYS.

VI.

THIS important part of the general future being thus successfully under way, the next thing was to fit up a pig-pen, for the new queen in the boys' affections would very soon be brought home. As there was a scarcity of materials on the farm for constructing a fashionable modern pen, with brick walls, shingle roof, plank floor, and costly iron feeding-trough, Uncle Benny directed them to use a large old molasses-hogshead, that happened to be lying idle. One of the boys got into it and removed all the projecting nails from the inside, then, placing it on its side, and blocking it so that it could not roll over, they put into it an abundant supply of straw for a bed. They then built a fence of old posts, broken rails, pieces of board, sticks from the wood-pile, and any other waste stuff they could find. In fact, there was nothing else to be had. It was a tottering, decrepit sort of affair, although strong enough to keep the pig in, but it enclosed sufficient room to give her a fine range, while the great hogshead would be sure to afford a retreat always dry and warm,—in fact, just such a shelter as a pig must have, if one expects him to keep himself clean and in thriving condition.

Though Uncle Benny had himself superintended the erection of a structure which was destined to be the theatre for very important events, yet, when finished, he gazed upon it with a sort of architectural dismay. He had a nice

man-farmer named Uncle Benny comes to rescue a struggling farm while in the process rescuing (or at least inspiring) a group of boys. *Farming for Boys* is set against the backdrop of rapid urbanization and industrialization, and indeed seeks to keep boys on the farm by making farm life seem exciting and meaningful. Meanwhile, other features reckoned with the joys of urban life, as well as life in other nations and on other continents.

Our Young Folks set a new standard in the quality of its writing and in its overall design, unmatched until *St. Nicholas* came along. Moreover, the magazine encouraged creative and critical thinking and fostered a sense of child-adult collaboration. Young readers were invited to participate and write back through its interactive features such as "Our Letter Box", "Young Competitors," and the "Mutual Improvement Corner." It's no coincidence that *Our Young Folks* was also passionately pro-Union and anti-slavery. We need look no further for material that celebrates children as thinkers and authors in their own right. In 1874, to Trowbridge's regret, *Our Young Folks* was sold to Scribner and Company and merged with the ascendant *St. Nicholas*, edited by Mary Mapes Dodge, author of *Hans Brinker or The Silver Skates*. Fortunately, Trowbridge and other contributors continued to write for *St. Nicholas*, which built upon and further improved the innovation and excellence of its predecessor, serializing many works now recognized as children's classics, including Frances Hodgson Burnett's *Little Lord Fauntleroy*.

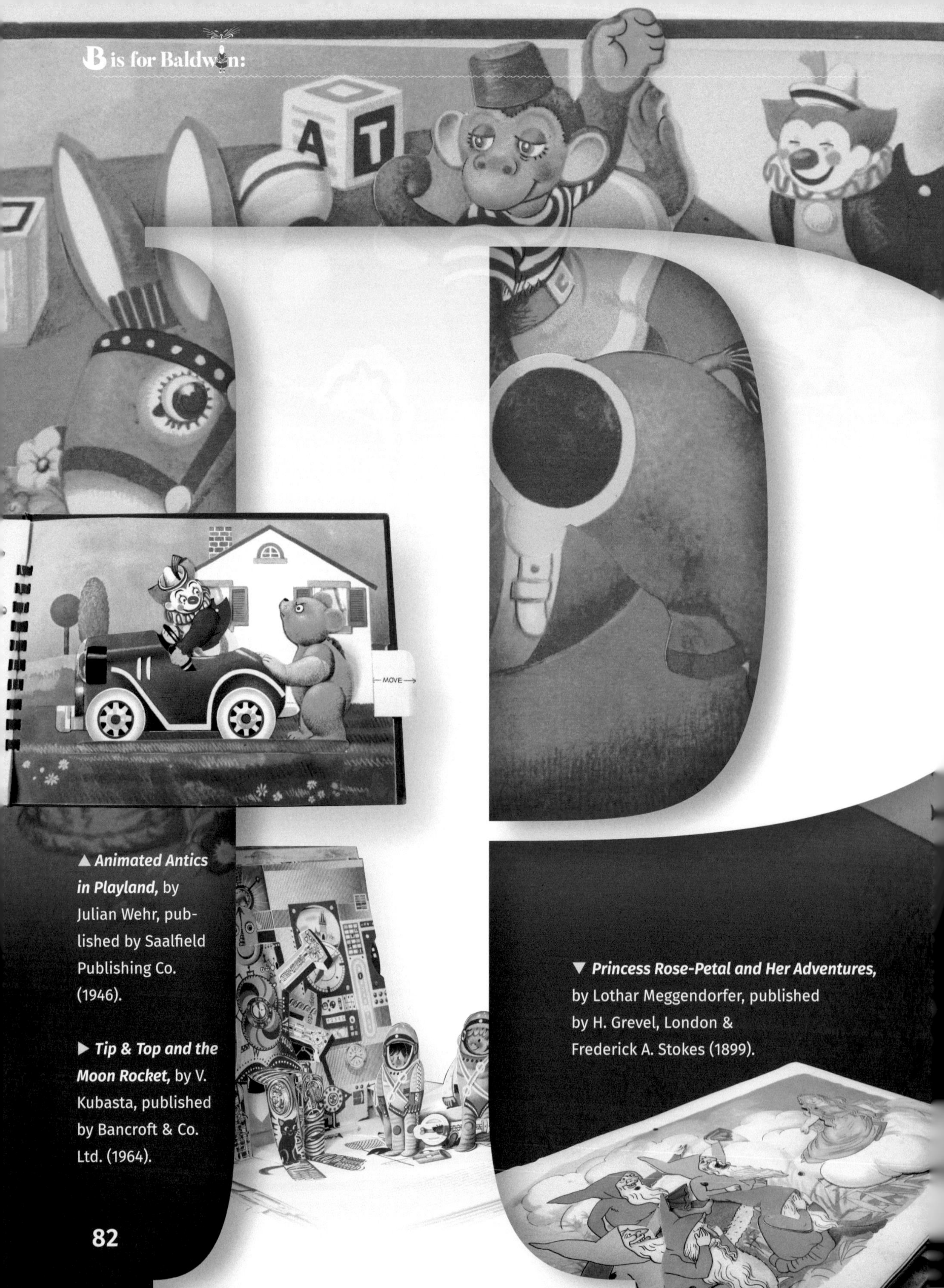

▲ ***Animated Antics in Playland,*** by Julian Wehr, published by Saalfield Publishing Co. (1946).

▶ ***Tip & Top and the Moon Rocket,*** by V. Kubasta, published by Bancroft & Co. Ltd. (1964).

▼ ***Princess Rose-Petal and Her Adventures,*** by Lothar Meggendorfer, published by H. Grevel, London & Frederick A. Stokes (1899).

Emily Brooks

is for Pop-Up

While the first instances of paper engineering in books are believed to be spinning disks (volvelles) used in astronomical texts in the 14th century, pop-ups today are popularly considered to be entertaining books for children.

The concept of childhood as a separate identity emerged in the seventeenth-century as society began to recognize that children required different learning and entertainment needs. Although toys used to be built from castoffs of craftsmen, by the 19th century, toys comprised its own industry. Toys, like the paper dolls seen in the intricately hand-colored

▲ ***ABC in Living Models,*** by S. Louis Gerard, published by Strand Publications (1935).

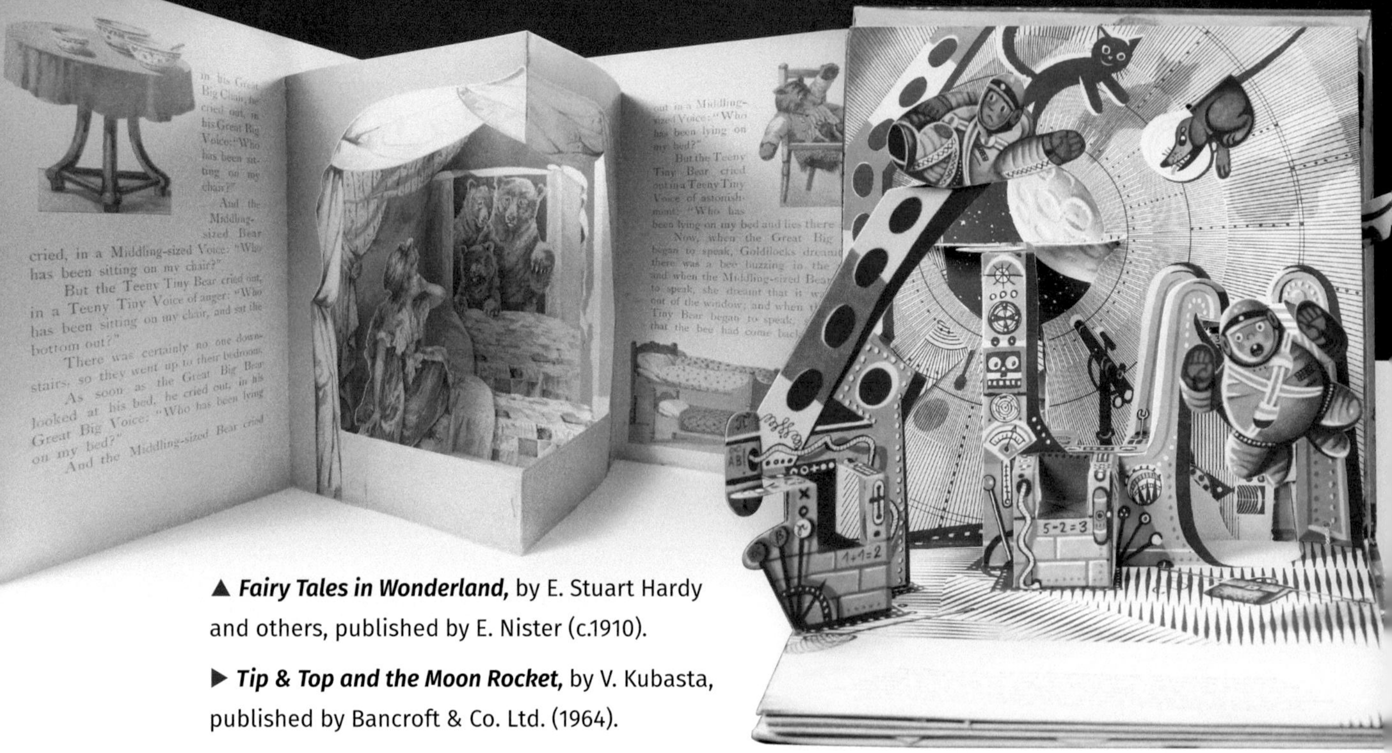

▲ ***Fairy Tales in Wonderland,*** by E. Stuart Hardy and others, published by E. Nister (c.1910).

▶ ***Tip & Top and the Moon Rocket,*** by V. Kubasta, published by Bancroft & Co. Ltd. (1964).

The History of Little Fanny, Exemplifed in a Series of Figures by S. and J. Fuller (1810), can be found in the Baldwin Library. As children's literature developed alongside new printing technologies, more innovations in the book form led to the golden age of movable books. The Baldwin houses an impressive assortment of pop-ups from some of the 19th century German and English masters, including *Dean's New Book of Dissolving Pictures* by Dean & Son (1862), *Always Jolly: A Movable Toybook* by Lothar Meggendorfer (1891), *Fun at the Circus* by Raphael Tuck & Sons (1892), and *Wild Animal Stories: a Panorama Picture Book* by Ernest Nister (1897). Emulating the style and stories of European pop-ups, the McLoughlin Brothers company was one of the first to produce pop-up books for American children. One early example in the Baldwin is the *Sleeping Beauty Pantomime* toy book (1870).

Movable book publishing experienced a lull around World War I as resources were diverted to aid in the war effort, but in the 1930s and 40s, a second renaissance of pop-up books flourished. Influences of popular culture and animation are evident in pop-ups at this time. Movables from some of the most recognized artists and companies of the time are represented in the collection, including *Bookano Zoo: Animals in Fact, Fancy and Fun* by S. Louis Giraud (1935), *The Exciting Adventures of Finnie the Fiddler* by Julian Wehr (1942), and *The "Pop-up" Minnie Mouse*, a collaboration of Walt Disney Studios and Blue Ribbon Books (1933). Though the influence of animation is evident in many movable books, the effects of art and architecture can also be seen in pop-up books. In the 1950s, Vojtech Kubasta, a

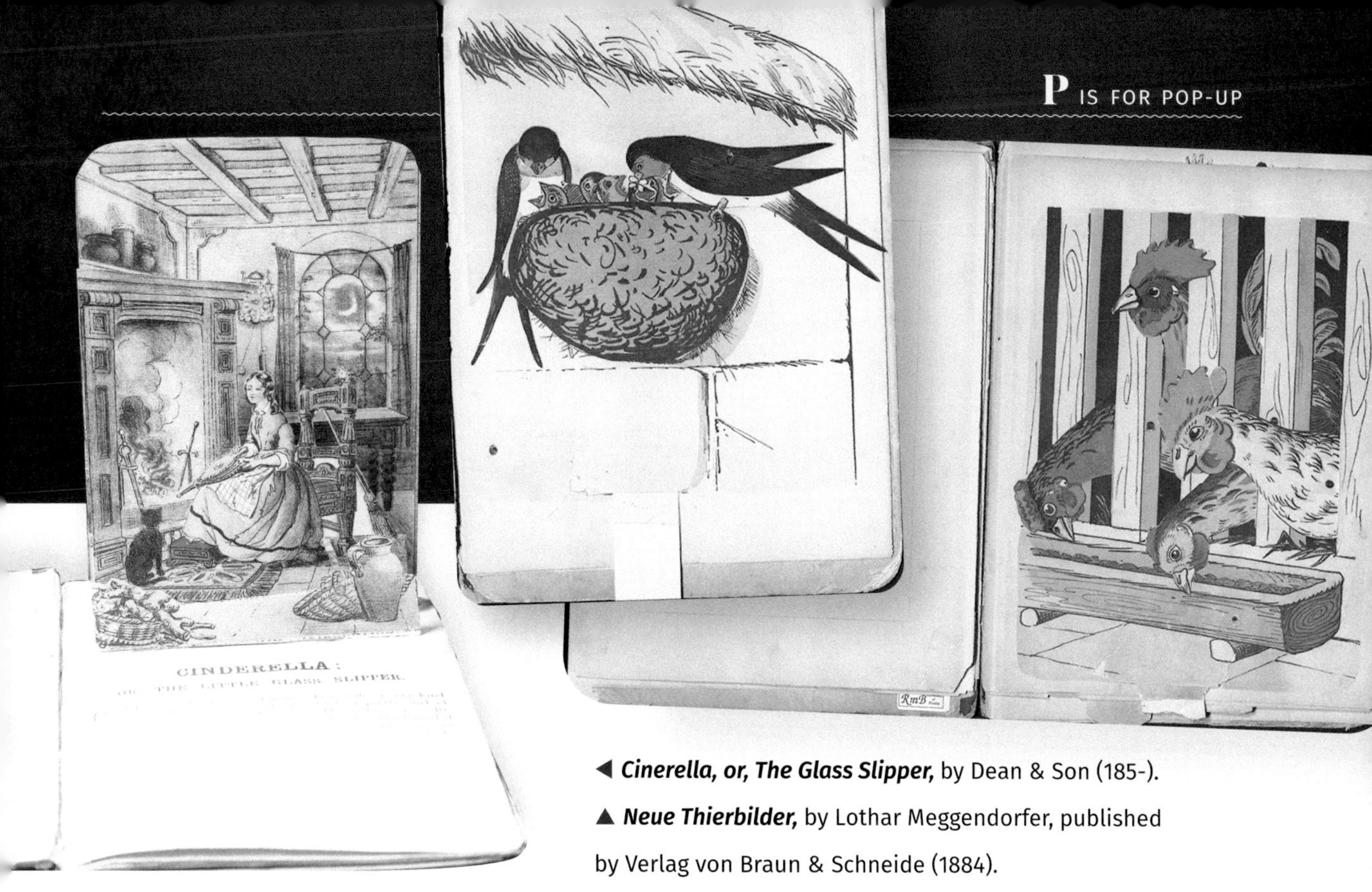

◀ ***Cinerella, or, The Glass Slipper,*** by Dean & Son (185-).

▲ ***Neue Thierbilder,*** by Lothar Meggendorfer, published by Verlag von Braun & Schneide (1884).

Prague architect and artist, submitted his first pop-up book to ARTIA, a Cold War-era government-run company. Since then, his books have been translated into over 20 languages and over 30 million copies have been sold. His books, like *Tip & Top and the Moon Rocket* (1964), are brilliant feats of paper engineering that push the boundaries of the page.

Technological progress in die-cutting, new paper-like materials, and varnishes in the late 20th and early 21st century allowed for developments of exquisite, sturdy, and remarkably inexpensive pop-up books. Some of my favorite contemporary paper engineers that I have adored since I was a child are featured in the Baldwin. Tor Lokvig, for example, has collaborated on an impressive array of texts including Jan Pienkowski's *Haunted House* (1979), Michael Bond's *Paddington Learns a Lesson* (1981), and Richard Scarry's *Mr. Frumble: Smallest Pop-up Book Ever* (1992). Other artists like David Carter, Robert Sabuda, and Matthew Reinhart have elevated pop-up books to collectible status. David Carter's *Color* series (e.g., *600 Black Spots*), for example, serves as a fascinating introduction to postmodern artists like Matisse and Mondrian. Some popular children's tales also serve as inspiration for Robert Sabuda's pop-ups, including C.S. Lewis' *The Chronicles of Narnia* (2007) or Tomie de Paola's *Brava, Strega Nona: a Heartwarming Pop-up Book* (2008), but Sabuda's pièce de résistance is his pop-up version of L. Frank Baum's *The Wonderful Wizard of Oz* (2000), complete with a spinning tornado, a holographic hot air balloon, and a secret message for those willing to follow the yellow brick road to the Emerald City.

QUEER
PEOPLE

AUTHOR
OF
THE BROWNIES

Kenneth Kidd

▲ ***Queer Pets at Marcy's,***
by Olive Thorne Miller, published by E.P. Dutton & Co. (c.1880).

Generally and in stories for children, "queer" has long meant the strange, the peculiar, the fantastic, the animal and the animal-affiliated.

is for Queer

E. H. Knatchbull-Hugessen's *Queer Folk: Seven Stories* (1874) features fairies and other magical creatures, "altogether as queer a collection of creatures as ever came together in a storybook," writes the author. And "if anyone objects to the title, I can only say that if he will write seven queerer stories, and find a better name for the book which contains them, I shall be very much obliged to him." Animals are queer in Harriet Beecher Stowe's *Queer Little People* (1867), Olive Thorne Miller's *Queer Pets at Marcy's* (1880), *Pussy's Queer Babies, and Other Stories* (1887), and Palmer Cox's *Queer People with Wings and Sting and Their Kweer Kapers* (1895). In some titles, royalty and queerness overlap, as in *The Queer Little Princess and Her Friends* (1888) and *Queer People Such as Goblins, Giants, Merry Men, and Monarchs* (1888). Edward Eggleston explains that his 1884 *Queer Stories for Boys and Girls* is a collection of stories "not entirely realistic in their setting, but appealing to the fancy, which is so marked a trait of the mind of girls and boys." Children, too, are queer, in part because they love queer creatures

◀ ***Queer People with Wings and Stings and Their Kweer Kapers,***
by Palmer Cox, published by Edgewood Publishing Company (c.1895).

THE HEN THAT HATCHED DUCKS.

A STORY.

ONCE there was a nice young hen that we will call Mrs. Feathertop. She was a hen of most excellent family, being a direct descendant of the Bolton Grays, and as pretty a young fowl as you should wish to see of a summer's day. She was, moreover, as fortunately situated in life as it was

1

▲ ***Queer Little People,*** by Harriet Beecher Stowe, published by Houghton Mifflin Co. (1909).

100 *QUEER PETS AT MARCY'S.*

The General was now about the size of a rat, and having survived the disasters of storm and hunger, became an important personage in the house. Like other people of his age, he was

THE GENERAL IN HIS NEW HOUSE.

fed on bread and milk, of which he was fond, was petted to his heart's content, and became perfectly tame, much more so than his mother had been.

His first cottage house having been destroyed by the storm,

▲ ***Queer Pets at Marcy's,*** by Olive Thorne Miller, published by E.P. Dutton & Co. (c.1880).

"YOU WILL STAND RIGHT THERE, LITTLE BOY!"

Page 30

▲ ***Queer Janet,*** by Grace LeBaron, published by Lee & Shepard Lothrop (1897).

THE FAIRIES AND THE CRUEL FARMER.

One night some fairies
sauntered round,
Within a farmer's
pasture ground;
And while on rocks
and hillocks green,
They paused to rest
and view the scene,
They held a sort of
running talk,
About the way he
used his stock.

▲ ***Queer People such as Goblins, Giants, Merry-men and Monarchs, and their Kweer Kapers,*** by Palmer Cox, published by Hubbard Brothers (c.1888).

and queer stories. Grace LeBaron opens her 1897 Christmas novel *Queer Janet* thus: "Queer Janet! Yes, that is what almost everyone called her! But her dear old grandmother, who loved her as only a grandmother can love, would always say of her,—'Janet is not like children in general;'—and it was grandmother who came nearest the truth" (1). Children are called "queer" in not a few children's classics, such as Frances Hodgson Burnett's *The Secret Garden* (1911), with its assorted eccentric children, and George MacDonald's fantasy *At the Back of the North Wind* (1871). In such works, the queer child stands out, mostly in good ways, and often undergoes a transformation and/or enables the transformations of others. Hubbard's Queer Person (that's his name), a "queer, pinched little soul," wanders into a Pikuni village as a small child, and is adopted by an "old hag" named Granny. Growing up, he "realized he was different from the rest [but] he did not know exactly what it was all about." With help from his grandmother and the village warriors, he learns sign language—inventing "a little style all his own"—then goes on a vision quest, after which he becomes a leader of the tribe. Stories such as these helped make "queer" part of public discourse. To be queer was unusual but not bad—often quite the contrary. Queer Janet is admirable in her goodness and originality, and Queer Person ends up a hero. By the early twentieth century, however, such usage tapered off, as queer came to mean something more sinister: non-heterosexual activity or identity. Queer became a slur. More recently, of course, the term has been rehabilitated, and contemporary queer literature for children—generally understood as LGBTQ material—harkens back to the more expansive usage of the late nineteenth and early twentieth centuries. Publishers for young readers aren't yet again embracing the titular queer, but that day might not be far off.

▲ ***Queer People such as Goblins, Giants, Merry-men and Monarchs, and their Kweer Kapers,*** by Palmer Cox, published by Hubbard Brothers (c.1888).

THE

LIFE

And moſt Surprizing

ADVENTURES

OF

ROBINSON CRUSOE, of

YORK, Mariner.

WHO

Lived Eight and Twenty Years in an Uninhabited Iſland on the Coaſt of *America*, lying near the Mouth of the Great River of *Oroonoque*: Having been caſt on Shore by Shipwreck, wherein all the Men were drowned, but Himſelf: As alſo a Relation how he was wonderfully deliver'd by Pyrates.

The whole Three Volumes faithfully Abridg'd, and ſet forth with Cuts proper to the Subject.

The SECOND EDITION.

LONDON:

Printed, For *A. Bettesworth*, at the *Red-Lyon* in *Pater-Noſter-Row*; *J. Brotherton* at the *Bible*, *W. Meadows* at the *Angel* in *Corn-Hill*; and *E. Midwinter*, at the *Looking-Glaſs* on *London-Bridge*. 1724.

"Going towards the boat I was exceedingly surprised with the print of a man's naked foot on the shore."

▲ ***Adventures of Robinson Crusoe,*** by Daniel Defoe, published by S. W. Partridge & Co. (1873).

▲ ▶ ***The Life and Strange Surprising Adventures of Robinson Crusoe, of York, Mariner,*** Frontispiece by John Clark and John Pine, published by W. Taylor (1719).

Terry Harpold

The Baldwin Library includes over 300 copies of Daniel Defoe's 1719 novel *The Life and Strange Surprising Adventures of Robinson Crusoe, of York, Marine.*

is for Robinson Crusoe

▲ ***The Life and Adventures of Robinson Crusoe,*** by Daniel Defoe, illustrated by Thomas Stothard, published by Ballantyne (1881).

▲ ***Adventures of Robinson Crusoe,*** by Daniel Defoe, published by John Bysh (183-).

ROBINSON CRUSOE.

EARLY LIFE.

1632,

▲ ***Robinson Crusoe in Pitman's Shorthand (Corresponding Style),*** by Daniel Defoe, published by Sir Isaac Pitman & Sons, Ltd. (1887).

ROBINSON CRUSOE

I STOOD LIKE ONE THUNDERSTRUCK

The oldest is a third edition, second state, published June 6, 1719. The book has been rebound, its pages are foxed and waterstained, but it is in otherwise good condition. The newest copies date from the 2010s. Most are from the nineteenth and early twentieth centuries, the golden age of the illustrated *Crusoe*.[i] Nearly all are readers' editions. Scholarly and critical editions are shelved in UF's general humanities collections; the Baldwin is home to the rare and unusual variants of the novel.

Here there are many abridged and rewritten versions, mostly board books and picture books for children, versions in rhyming verse and in words of one syllable, and a version in Basic English, a grammatically-simplified, 850-word subset of the language. Another transcribes Defoe's text into Pitman Shorthand. Bowdlerized versions emphasize religious elements of the novel or delete scenes of violence. (An editor's note observes, "nothing is said of the cannibal savages. The record of such scenes is not fit for any of our 'early' readers.")

Most abridged and unabridged editions in the collection are illustrated, many by celebrated artists, including Elenor Plaisted Abbott, C.E. Brock, George Cruikshank, J.J. Grandville, Ernest Henry Griset, Walter Paget, Lewis and Frederick Rhead, Thomas Stothard, and N.C. Wyeth. (Someone has written in pencil on the front endpaper of the 1900 edition illustrated by the Rhead brothers, "[American book illustrator] Howard Pyle called this 'the most beautiful book of the generation.'") Several editions include maps of Crusoe's "Island of Despair." In a few, readers have added original touches of color to black and white images with crayon, pencil, and paint.

Other copies include tipped-in advertisements for consumer products, e.g., Fry's Pure Concentrated Cocoa, "unsurpassed for purity, solubility, and perfection"—not to be confused with Armbrecht's Coca Wine, "made from the best Peruvian coca leaves" and good for treating influenza, sleeplessness, and

◀ ***The Life and Strange Surprising Adventures of Robinson Crusoe, of York, Mariner,*** illustrated by Louis Rhead and Frederick Alfred Rhead, published by R. H. Russell (1900).

"brainfag." ("A wineglassful taken twice a day is recommended. Children should take "half or a quarter of this quantity.")

Parents, relatives, and schoolteachers have often promoted Crusoe's example of perseverance and self-reliance to young readers. Many of the copies feature encouraging inscriptions: "From Mr. and Mrs. Campbell with their affectionate love to Henry Stuart Murray, Edinburgh, 9th Sept. 1868," "A Birthday present to Harry Morgan Gilmour from his father. April 18th 1893"; "To Harry Gates from Grandmother Gates / Christmas 1914"; "G.O. Cowan / Second Prize, in Class III," "A Prize for Attendance and Lessons during the year 1872;" "As a reward for spelling this is presented to Master Ira Ricks by Miss Emma Lown, Teacher." (Added below, a gentle reminder: "Be diligent E.L.")

Bookplates figure more formal signs of a copy's provenance. Most of the Baldwin's copies of *Crusoe* with plates are straightforward *ex libris* warnings to borrowers and would-be thieves. A few hint at wider prospects: *Lux e tenebris* ("Light out of darkness," a Masonic motto), *Pereunt cetera litterae manent* ("Other things perish, literature endures.")

The most compelling of the bookplates is in a well-preserved 1895 edition published by Ernest Nister and E.P. Dutton, which declares the book a prize awarded on May 15, 1897 by the Royal Society for the Prevention of Cruelty to Animals to James Lyell Ritchie, for his essay on "Man's Duty Toward Animals." I've long been fascinated by this unusual evidence of a book's journey to the Baldwin and I've searched for other traces of James Lyell Ritchie in surviving government archives and family records, with limited success.

He was born in Islington, Middlesex, in 1883 or 1884. He was thirteen when he won this copy of *Crusoe* for the best original essay by a pupil of the Sherbrooke Road Board School, Fulham. Out of the 139,326 essays submitted to the contest by pupils of London area schools, only 1,446 were awarded a prize.[ii]

▲ ***The Life and Adventures of Robinson Crusoe,*** by Daniel Defoe, illustrated by John Dawson Watson, published by George Routledge and Sons (1891).

"I stood like one thunderstruck." (See p. 180.)

▲ ***Adventures of Robinson Crusoe,*** by Daniel Defoe, illustrated by J.J. Grandville, John Proctor, and others, published by Henry Lea (1880).

[i] Blewett, David. *The Illustration of Robinson Crusoe, 1719–1920.* Colin Smythe, 1995.

[ii] Royal Society for the Prevention of Cruelty to Animals. "Distribution of Prizes in the Crystal Palace." *The Animal World,* June 1, 1897: 90–99, 102.

His parents were born in Forfarshire, Scotland; his father was a traveling salesman, his mother probably a homemaker. A sister, Dora, was born in 1889 or 1890, in Manor Park. By 1911, James was living with his parents in Catford and working as an insurance clerk. Dora had become a schoolmistress and had recently moved out of the family home.

In the spring of 1918, at the age of 34, James was a Private in the Horse Transport Branch of the 6th (Service) Battalion, The Buffs (East Kent Regiment). He may have been conscripted a year or two before. By late March, the 6th Buffs were caught up in the brutal trench warfare near Amiens, France, where Allied troops succeeded, at huge cost, in halting the German Spring Offensive. James was killed on March 28, 1918 in the First Battle of Arras, near the hamlet of Mesnil, along the Ancre River between Albert and Hamel. His body was not recovered. His name and rank appear on the Pozières Memorial, France, along with those of 14,656 other missing British and South African soldiers killed that spring.

Royal Society for the Prevention of Cruelty to Animals.

Patrons:

Her Most Gracious Majesty the Queen.
H.R.H the Prince of Wales, H.R.H. the Princess of Wales, H.R.H. the Duke, and H.R. and I.H. the Duchess of Edinburgh, H.R.H. the Duke of Connaught, H.R.H. the Duchess of Connaught, H.R.H. Prince Christian, H.R.H. Princess Christian, H.R.H. the Princess Louise, H.R.H. the Princess Henry of Battenberg, H.R.H. the Duchess of Albany, H.R.H. the Duke of Cambridge, H.R.H. the Duchess of Teck, H.H. the Duke of Teck, H.R.H. the Princess Frederica, Baron von Pawel Rammingen, H.S.H. Prince Edward of Saxe-Weimar, H.S.H. Princess Edward of Saxe-Weimar

President:—His Royal Highness the Duke of York, K.G

President of the Ladies' Committee:—Rt Hon. Baroness Burdett-Coutts.

This Volume is awarded to

James L. Ritchie

for an Essay on "Man's Duty towards Animals," and presented at the Crystal Palace, May 15th, 1897.

Jno Colam

Secretary, 105, Jermyn St., London.

Diamond Jubilee, 1897.

▲ Bookplate from ***The Life and Strange Adventures of Robinson Crusoe of York, Mariner,*** by Ernest Nister, published by E.P. Dutton (1895).

" Having learned to know the value of retirement, and the blessing of ending our days in peace."

▲ ***Adventures of Robinson Crusoe,*** by Daniel Defoe, published by S. W. Partridge & Co (1873).

CRUSOE.
Plate 5.
Robinson Crusoe's Calendar. He every day cut a notch in his post.
page 72.

▲ ***Robinson Crusoe,*** by Daniel Defoe, published by J. Harris and Son (1821).

His father David died later that year, his mother Eliza in 1939. The family gravestone in Hither Green Cemetery, Lewisham, memorializes the parents and James. In 1926, Dora married a schoolmaster, Raymond Arthur Howard Scannell. Raymond died in 1965, and Dora in 1970. Their daughter Jean, born in 1927, married Brian Howard Padgham in 1957. Jean and Brian died in 2010, by which time this copy of *Crusoe* was already in the Baldwin collection. When and how it arrived in Gainesville, very far from Islington, Lewisham, and Mesnil, is unknown.

On one day in May 1897, a young working class boy's compassion for his fellow creatures was celebrated from the platform of the Crystal Palace before an audience of 30,000 spectators. Otherwise, James Lyell Ritchie's life up to the moment of his cruel death appears to have been as modest and unremarkable as the lives of many thousands of other souls sacrificed in the first War to End All Wars. Apart from the most banal government records, only a surname and two initials on Panel 16 of the Pozières Memorial, four terse lines on a family gravestone, and this bookplate endure as witnesses to his brief life.

▶ ***Aunt Jane's Verses for Children,*** by T. D. Crewdson, illustrated by Henry Anelay, published by Charles Gilpin (1851).

Ramona Caponegro

Since Ruth Baldwin collected "the volumes that were loved and read by children and so ordinary that no else collected them", it is hardly surprising that series books abound in the Baldwin Library.[i]

The Aunt Jane's Nieces Series

BOOKS FOR GIRLS

By EDITH VAN DYNE

NINE TITLES

Aunt Jane's Nieces
Aunt Jane's Nieces Abroad
Aunt Jane's Nieces at Millville
Aunt Jane's Nieces at Work
Aunt Jane's Nieces in Society
Aunt Jane's Nieces and Uncle John
Aunt Jane's Nieces on Vacation
Aunt Jane's Nieces on the Ranch
Aunt Jane's Nieces Out West

DISTINCTLY girls' books and yet stories that will appeal to *brother* as well—and to older folk. Real and vital—rousing stories of the experiences and exploits of three real girls who do things. Without being sensational, Mrs. Van Dyne has succeeded in writing a series of stories that have the tug and stir of fresh young blood in them. Each story is complete in itself.

Illustrated 12mo. Uniform cloth binding, stamped in colors, with beautiful colored inlay. Fancy colored jackets. Price 60 cents each.

Publishers The Reilly & Britton Co. Chicago

▲ ***Aunt Jane's Nieces Out West,*** by L. Frank Baum, illustrated by James McCracken, published by Reilly & Britton Co. (1914).

is for Series Books

As Paul Deane declares, "We can safely assume that in the realm of children's literature, series are the most widely read books."[ii] Their popularity stems from multiple factors, including their comforting familiarity, ubiquity, and appeal to the collecting desire. Series books typically feature the same characters, are created by the same author or syndicate, and have a consistent and recognizable format. They are written in almost every genre, fiction and nonfiction, with each series marketed as a set of titles that may contain standalone stories but should ideally be read (and bought) in a certain order or as part of a collection.

▲ ***Ruth Fielding In the Great Northwest,*** **by Alice B. Emerson, published by Cupples & Leon Co. (1921).**

Despite—or perhaps because of—their popularity with young readers, series have a contested place within children's literature. As Kathleen Chamberlain asserts, "The accepted scholarly wisdom is that series books in general have been dismissed by most adults as mediocre time-wasters at best and harmful mind-warpers at worst. Although this view is not completely accurate, it does represent a typical critical response, especially toward those series perceived to be hastily written, mass-produced, or 'sensational' and unrealistic."[iii] Nevertheless, readers return to series books to revisit beloved worlds, grow with characters, engage in favorite subjects, and check off new titles in the series' lists.

The Baldwin Library contains thousands of titles from famous and obscure series. Jacob Abbott receives credit for creating the first American children's book series, launched in 1835 with *The Little Scholar Learning to Talk* (later retitled *Rollo Learning to Talk*). The individual *Rollo* books were first promoted as a series in 1839, and the first series about Rollo led to a second series about him, as well as two companion series.[iv] The Baldwin has multiple editions of all 14 books in the first *Rollo* series and all 10 books in the *Rollo's Tour of Europe* series. It also has numerous volumes of the famed Nancy Drew Mystery Stories, beginning with the inaugural title, *The Secret of the Old Clock* (1930), as well as all 10 books of the little-remembered *Aunt Jane's Nieces* series (1906-1918), penned under a pseudonym by L. Frank Baum, best known for his Oz books. In addition to character-based series, the collection holds hundreds of books from brand-based series, such as the Big Little Books (See "L is for Little Books for Little Hands") and Little Golden Books (see "G is for Golden Books"). Most popular in the 1930s and 1940s, the Big Little Books and imitating series are easily identified by their small size, pairing of a captioned illustration with nearly every page of text, and content rooted in popular culture, particularly films, comics, and radio programs. A look through the Baldwin's holdings reveals many more series books, a testament to their longstanding popularity with young readers.

[i] Smith, Rita J. "Caught Up in the Whirlwind: Ruth Baldwin." *The Lion and the Unicorn* 22.3 (September 1998): 300.

[ii] Deane, Paul. *Mirrors of American Culture: Children's Fiction Series in the Twentieth Century.* Metuchen, NJ, and London: Scarecrow, 1991. 5.

[iii] Chamberlain, Kathleen. "'Wise Censorship': Cultural Authority and the Scorning of Juvenile Series Books, 1890-1940." *Scorned Literature: Essays on the History and Criticism of Popular Mass-Produced Fiction in America.* Eds. Lydia Cushman Schurman and Deidre Johnson. Westport, CT: Greenwood, 2002. 188.

[iv] Johnson, Deirdre. "From Abbott to Animorphs, from Godly Books to Goosebumps: The Nineteenth-Century Origins of Modern Series." *Scorned Literature: Essays on the History and Criticism of Popular Mass-Produced Fiction in America.* Eds. Lydia Cushman Schurman and Deidre Johnson. Westport, CT: Greenwood, 2002. 148-9.

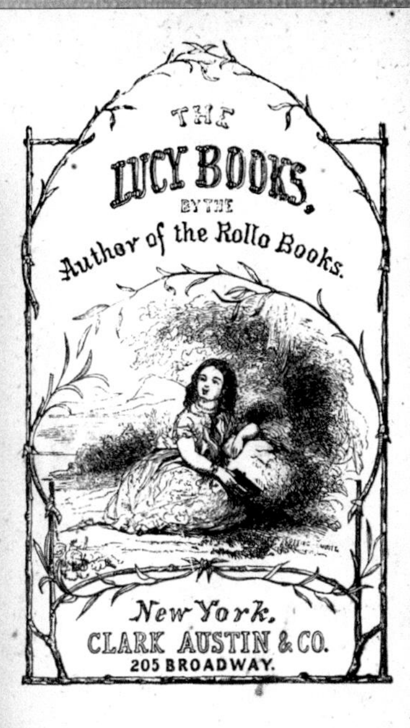

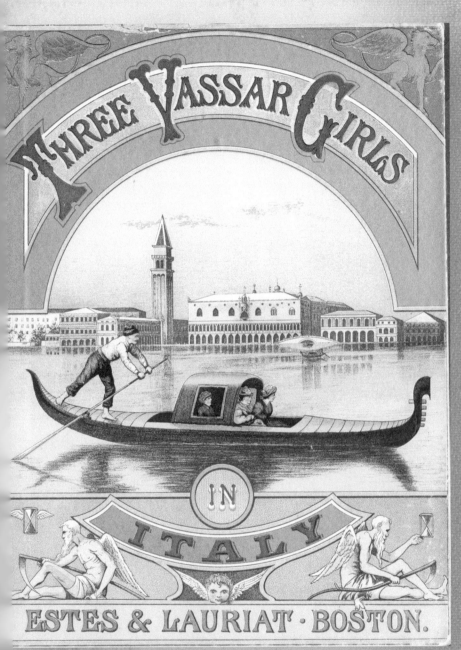

▲ ***Cousin Lucy Among the Mountains,*** by Jacob Abbott, published by Clark, Austin & Co. (1852).

▲ ***Three Vassar Girls in Italy,*** by Elizabeth Champney, illustrated by James Wells Champney, published by Estes & Lauriat (1885).

► ***The Secret of the Old Clock (Nancy Drew, Book 1),*** by Carolyn Keene, illustrated by Russell H. Tandy, published by Grosset & Dunlap (1930).

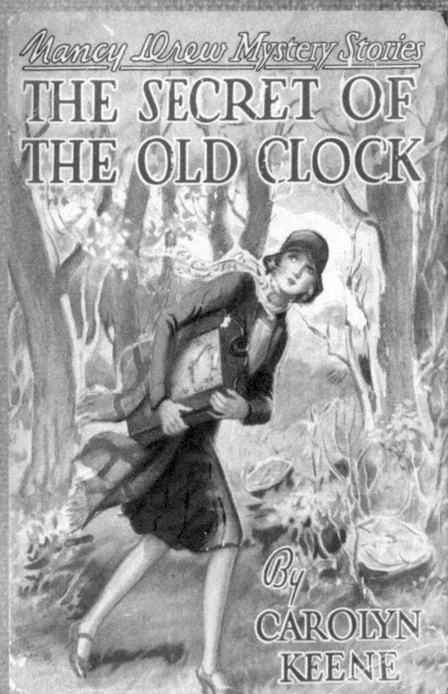

▲▶ ***The Speaking Picture Book: A Special Book with Picture Rhyme & Sound for Little People,*** by Theodor Brand (c.1893).

T is for Talking Books

Jill Coste

From phonics to phonetics, talking books can encompass a variety of meanings, and the Baldwin Library has examples of them all.

▲ ***Rollo Learning to Talk,*** by Jacob Abbott, published by Sheldon & Company (1865).

The Speaking Picture Book

A new Picture Book with characteristic Voices

Printed in Germany

The collection has no small selection of books about learning to talk. The early readers are of particular note, with their delicate yellowed pages offering instruction not just to children but to their parents as well. "[R]ead in a very animated tone of voice, and with marked intonations and inflections," urge the instructions in Jacob Abbott's *Learning to Talk; or, Entertaining and Instructive Lessons in the Use of Language* (ix). Similarly, the narrator in *Rollo Learning to Talk*, also by Jacob Abbott, suggests that "[t]hese little talks about pictures are mainly intended to be read by a mother…to a little one who is learning to talk" and encourages the reader to "act out all the motions described" (1). Similarly, Dorothy Kilner's 1801 publication, *The Rational Brutes, or Talking Animals* features a mother who teaches her young children lessons about acceptance and respect through stories of talking animals.

Talking animals appear in numerous other texts, usually making beastie sounds as tools for readers to learn animal names. The 1981 *Animal Sounds* features a way for children to practice their own animal utterances, as young readers encounter bright illustrations and directions that "The cow says 'Moo-o-o-o" and chickens say "Cluck, cluck." A 1955 text called *The Talking Animal Book* offers something similar, but with oblong pages that bulge where readers can press a button to elicit an ostensible animal noise. Either from age or construction, the buttons—three in all—produce a simple toy squeaker sound, nothing close to imitating the actual "baa," "quack," or "chirp" produced by an animal.

NOTICE TO PARENT

THESE little talks about pictures are ma
ended to be read by a mother, or by one
lder children, to a little one who is learni
alk. Their design is to interest and amus

10

FEEDING THE CHICKENS.

Here is a picture of a little girl feeding the chickens. Little girl! * Little

girl, did you know that you had left the gate open? Little girl, I say, *little girl*, did you know that you had left the gate open? She does not know

* Call "Little girl!" in the tone you would use if you really expected an answer, and pause a moment for a reply. So in all similar cases.

▲▶ ***Rollo Learning to Talk***, by Jacob Abbott, published by Sheldon & Company (1865).

But there is a spectacular text in the Baldwin that *does* make these sounds, and remarkably well for a pull-string contraption fashioned in the late 19th century. *The Speaking Picture Book*, first published in German in 1880 and reproduced for F.A.O. Schwartz for sale in America circa 1890, is a gorgeous tome, rich with color illustrations. Its red fabric cover is embellished with a vivid illustration that should evoke comparison to *A Midsummer Night's Dream*, and mesh speakers peek from behind carved, gold-painted leaves. Though thick, the book has just 22 pages of text; the primary bulk of the book is comprised of the sound mechanism. This is the original Talking Book, with a charming rhyme that accompanies each featured animal and a pull string, tabbed with an ivory knob, for young readers to tug to create the animal sound. Rooster, donkey, lamb, birds, cow, cuckoo, and goat all get their own poem, illustration, and sound, though some sounds work better than others. The donkey gets a good "hee-haw," the lamb a sweet little "baa." The cow's lowing "moo" is surprisingly rich in tone, while the cuckoo mimics the sound of its namesake clock. The highlight of the sounds, though, is the goat—the pull mechanism judders in anticipation of the way it will jitter back into the book, drawing with it the unique, high-pitched stutter of a goat's cry. *The Speaking Picture Book* is a delight to experience and a masterpiece of Talking Books.

▲ ***The Rational Brutes, or Talking Animals,*** by Dorothy Kilner, published by B. & J. Johnson (1801).

Hélène Huet & Suzan Alteri

Le Spectacle Asiatique Danse et Voltige sur la Corde avec sans Balancier **is a hand-colored tightrope toy and toy theater created in the summer of 1835 by J. Pintard in Paris.**

is for Unusual

It arrives from the stacks in an unassuming color-patterned paper folio that is folded and tied in the middle with a piece of twine. Inside *Le Spectacle Asiatique*, one finds a tightrope assemblage, a stage made of two parts: a raised stage floor and a five-panel stage background and 13 movable paper characters. The stage is meant to represent both the exoticism of the "Orient," as it was termed then, and its luxury as well as the elegant architecture of the Renaissance, to remind spectators of France. The characters one can use for the show include two French dancers, two Chinese dancers (a man and a woman), a genie, a sylph, a dwarf jester, a bayadère (Hindu dancer),

and two enslaved Ethiopians. The sylph, dwarf, and bayadère are the only three who can still move both their arms along with their legs.

Detailed instructions let the user in on the theater's secret—that only they can give life and movement to the paper characters, making them jump, dance, and walk on the tightrope seamlessly without any apparent aid. To achieve this goal, there is a tiny, weighted plastic line that runs along the top of the theater on which the characters carefully balance. If spectators are placed at a reasonable distance from the stage, it appears as if the characters are dancing in thin air. The owner of the *Spectacle* is also the stage director and needs to make people believe the characters are moving and dancing magically. This toy is all about skills, subtlety, and illusion.

Movables and paper illusions were a mainstay of children's literature throughout the nineteenth century and the Baldwin Library has an incredible collection of movable books, peep shows, magnetic toys and one-of-a-kind items like *Le Spectacle Asiatique* (The Baldwin Library has the only known recorded copy). Since animation and mechanical toys were still far in the future, booksellers and paper merchants relied on elaborate paper illusions to trick the eye into seeing something magical.

The toy theater was sold in the 1840s-1850s by La Maison Aubert for 26 francs under the "moveable caricatures" category in their catalogue. La Maison Aubert was a store owned by the lithographer, caricaturist, and journalist Charles Philipon, famous for being the editor of *La Caricature* and of *Le Charivari*, two satirical political journals. Philipon's Maison Aubert "dominated the production and distribution of caricatures in Paris in the mid-nineteenth century." In addition to selling caricatures, it sold toys which were connected to the art of drawing, of which *Le Spectacle Asiatique* was a spectacular example.

Photo credit: Tracy E. MacKay-Ratliff

Cuno, James. "Charles Philipon, La Maison Aubert, and the Business of Caricature in Paris, 1829-41." *Art Journal*, no. 4, 1983, pp. 347-55.

▲ ***Denslow's ABC Book,*** by W. W. Denslow, published by G.W. Dillingham Co. (1903).

BOSTON
TICKNOR AND COMPANY
211 Tremont Street
1889

THE DEAD DOLL.

◀ ***Dead Doll and Other Verses,*** by Margaret Vandegrift, published Ticknor & Co. (1889).

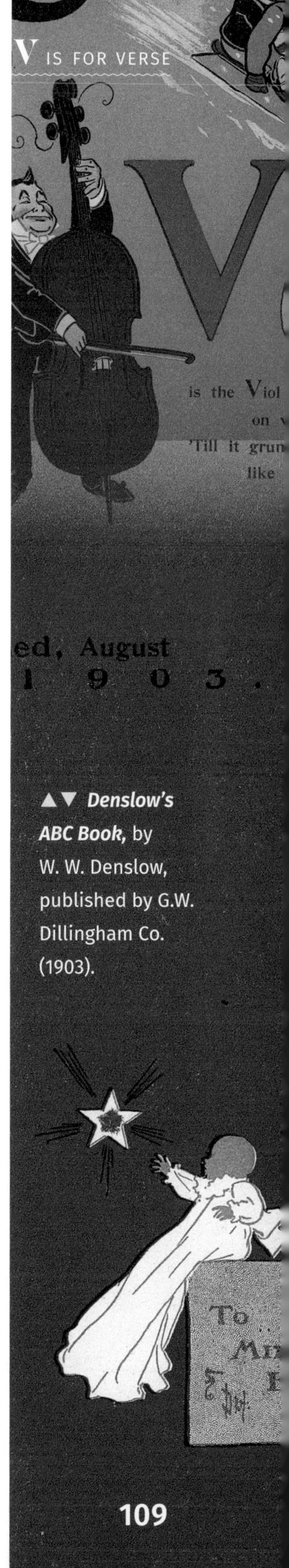

▲▼ ***Denslow's ABC Book,*** by W. W. Denslow, published by G.W. Dillingham Co. (1903).

is for Verse

Richard Flynn

Derived from the "Latin *versus* a line or row, spec. a line of writing (so named from turning to begin another line)," *verse*, according to the Oxford English Dictionary, describes a "metrical composition, form, or structure; language or literary work written or spoken in metre."

While its meter (and often rhyme) distinguishes it from *prose*, *verse* is often used pejoratively to imply that it is doggerel, and therefore opposed to *poetry*. Verse is central to children's literature and culture prior to 1920, as Angela Sorby has ably demonstrated in both her monograph *Schoolroom Poets* and her anthology, *Over the River and Through the Wood*, co-edited with Karen Kilcup. Yet the association of *verse* with children's literature may well be a reason it is devalued by adult poetry communities.

Certainly, there is some verse that qualifies as poetry in the over 1,400 digitized collections of poetry in the Baldwin, and the extensive digital collection of *St. Nicholas* magazine contains a wide variety of verse, much of it excellent. But not all the magazine's content is distinguished. As Sorby explains, its editor, Mary Mapes Dodge, created a hierarchy in the magazine of "'poems' (important, valuable, virtuous) 'verses' (less important, less valuable, less virtuous) [and] 'jingles' (not important, not valuable, not virtuous)." (72). While the Baldwin does house a collection of Dodge's original verse, *When Life is Young: A Collection of Verse for Boys and Girls* (1894), most of its poetry collections are not so prestigious. For instance, the title poem of Margaret Vandegrift's *The Dead Doll and Other Verses* (1888) features a young girl's insistent monologue which begins "You needn't be trying to comfort me —I tell you my dolly is dead! / There's no use in saying she isn't, with a crack like that in her head."

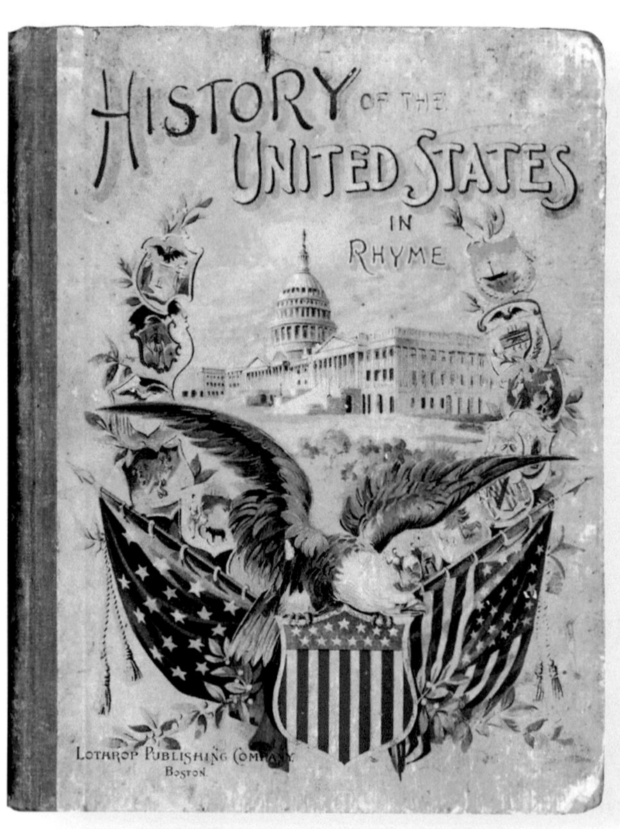

▲ ***History of the United States in Rhyme,*** by Robert C. Adams, published Lothrop Publishing Co. (c.1884).

I'll admit that while I derive more pleasure from the ridiculous than from the sublime, there are examples of both in the various subcategories of verse. The familiar style of the illustrations in *Denslow's ABC Book* (1903) render the alphabet verse therein charming; the stentorian claims of *The Temperance Alphabet for Bands of Hope* ("A stands for ALCOHOL. What is this? you inquire:/'Tis the Demon of Drink! the Spirit of Fire) are unintentionally amusing. The brilliant nonsense verse of Edward Lear is well represented, but more striking are oddities such as *Ye Book of Sense* (1878) and the relatively pedestrian *Nonsense for Girls* (c.1880). Animal verse includes Oliver Goldsmith's satire *Elegy on the Death of a Mad Dog,* illustrated by Randolph Caldecott, but for sheer camp value, it is hard to beat *The Good Dogs Who Always Did as They Were Bid* (1874). Nursery verse abounds—there are numerous "Three Little Kittens"—but I was fascinated by L. Frank Baum's and W.W. Denslow's *Father Goose: His Book,* and more than a little shocked by its casual racism, something that appears in a number of the other titles.

Most striking to me are the utilitarian verses one can barely imagine existing in the present. The mnemonic properties of verse are enlisted in *History of the United States in Rhyme* (1884) which offers "the student pressed for time/This condensation clothed in rhyme/ Tis hoped will prove a blessing." Likewise, Shakespeare is rendered in easy ballad stanzas in the British series *Tales of Shakespeare in Verse* (c.1880).

Regardless of its varying quality, verse performed a great deal of cultural work in England and America before the mid-twentieth century, and that contained in collections such as the Baldwin may provide many valuable traces for the serious scholar and the literary and cultural historian. If the verse also provides fodder for amusement, consider how our own popular verse forms—the verse-novel for the young, for instance—may amuse literary sleuths of future centuries.

▲▼ ***Good Dogs Who Alwys Did As They Were Bid,*** created and published by Thomas Nelson & Sons (1874).

▲ ***Lives of Girls Who Became Famous,*** by Sarah K. Bolton, published by Thomas Y. Crowell & Co. (c.1886).

▶ ***Heroes and Heroines,*** by Eleanor and Herbert Farjean, illustrated by Rosalind Thornycroft, published by E. P. Dutton & Co., Inc. (c.1940).

is for Women

Mary Roca

▲ ***A Child's Book of Saints,*** by William Canton, illustrated by Thomas Hastings Robinson, published by J. M. Dent & Co. (c.1886).

Women have long been associated with children's literature, in part because of cultural assumptions that writing for children is akin to caring for them—making children's literature a "natural" extension of women's roles.

This connection both reflected and created children's literature's marginalized status, as women could enter child-related fields largely because such work was deemed less important or challenging than men's work. Their resulting dominance in those fields reinforced not only the work's lesser status, but also the idea that womanhood and motherhood were synonymous. Even so, when women were barred from professional status in most fields, they could write, publish, evaluate, and collect children's literature—shaping the genre while elevating their positions within it. Children's literature offered, and continues to offer, women space to express themselves, build careers, and enact social change. The Baldwin Library reflects the impact one woman can have, both in Ruth Baldwin's collecting and in the countless women's work housed in the collection.

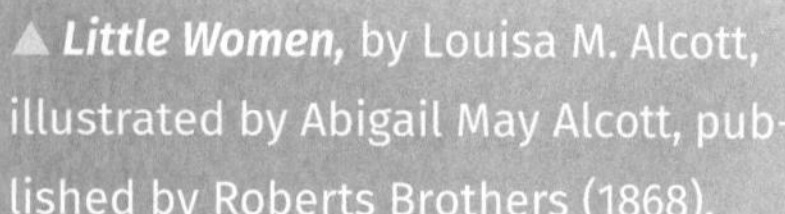

They all drew to the fire, mother in the big chair, with Beth at her feet; Meg and Amy perched on either arm of the chair, and Jo leaning on the back. — PAGE 12.

▲ ***Little Women,*** by Louisa M. Alcott, illustrated by Abigail May Alcott, published by Roberts Brothers (1868).

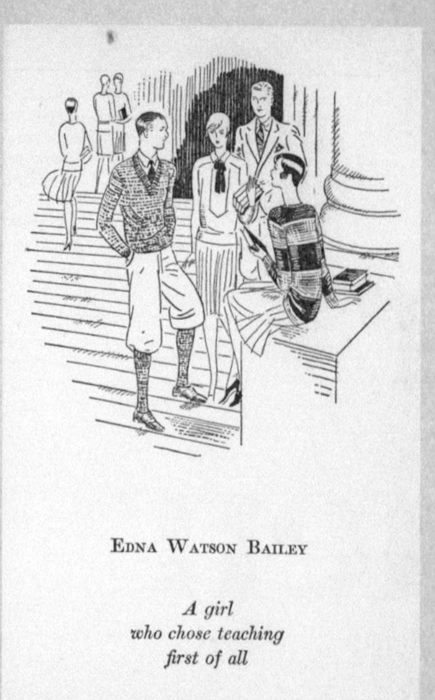

EDNA WATSON BAILEY
A girl
who chose teaching
first of all

▲ ***Girls Who Did,*** by Helen Josephine Ferris & Virginia Moore, illustrated by Harriet Moncure, published by E. P. Dutton & Co. (c.1927).

"What's the matter, Margery?"
"Nothing. I'm just waiting."
(See page 13)

▲ ***Little Question in Ladies' Rights,*** by Parker Fillmore, illustrated by Rose Cecil O'Neill, published by John Lane Co. (c.1927).

The Baldwin Library features women who impacted not only children's literature, but women's social and political positions more broadly. Louisa May Alcott published *Little Women* in 1868, sparking a girls' book market in response to the popularity of boys' books in the latter nineteenth century. *Little Women* marked the beginning of the girls' book, and remains a beloved text a century and a half later. The Baldwin Library reflects Alcott's popularity, as it preserves her works—including over two dozen editions of *Little Women*—as well as works about her. Similarly, the collection contains works by women like Lydia Maria Child, who among other accomplishments edited the children's magazine *Juvenile Miscellany*; Rose Cecil O'Neill, the first woman commercial illustrator in the U.S.; and Beatrix Potter, who was equal parts the creator of Peter Rabbit and respected natural scientist. The Baldwin Library contains countless examples of women's work: from hundreds of texts by prolific writers like Mary Martha Sherwood to books about women, like Sarah Josepha Hale's *Lessons from Women's Lives*, Sarah K. Bolton's *Lives of Girls Who Became Famous*, and Helen Josephine Ferris and Virginia Moore's *Girls Who Did: Stories of Real Girls and Their Careers*, among others.

As the Baldwin Library spans the seventeenth through the twenty-first centuries, it also documents women's work across time, through multiple editions, different revisions and retellings, and new books returning to the past. Biographies about Harriet Tubman are one example. The earliest, Sarah H. Bradford's *Harriet Tubman, the Moses of her People*, was originally

▼ ***Harriet and The Promised Land,*** by Jacob Lawrence, published by Simon & Schuster (1967 below & 1997 cover illustration in background).

published in 1869, expanded in 1886, and republished by Corinth Books in 1961. Unlike Bradford's biography, Hildegarde Hoyt Swift's *The Railroad to Freedom* (1932) was written for children, as were Ann Petry's *Harriet Tubman: Conductor on the Underground Railroad* (1955) and Sam and Beryl Epstein's *Harriet Tubman: Guide to Freedom* (1968). Jacob Lawrence's *Harriet and the Promised Land* (1968) is in verse, while later biographies emphasize different aspects of her life—Alan Schroeder's *Minty: A Story of Young Harriet Tubman* (1996) focuses on Tubman's girlhood and Carole Boston Weatherford's *Moses: When Harriet Tubman Led Her People to Freedom* (2007) highlights her spiritualism. As these texts retell and reimagine Harriet Tubman's life, the Baldwin Library preserves her history—and hundreds of other women's histories—for future generations.

Women have forged long-lasting and impactful careers through their work related to children's literature, translating the social association with children to a wide variety of fields. Thanks to Ruth Baldwin's work, and other women's work, the Baldwin Library is one of the strongest historical children's literature collections in the United States. As it expands, the collection will continue to document women and their work.

▶ ***Little Boys and Girls ABC,***
by McLoughlin Bros. (c.1884).

X xerxes. Y yacht. Z ze

Cari Keebaugh

X is for Xerxes, a character who has helped to teach children their alphabet for centuries.

is for Xerxes

His debut was in the famous British alphabet rhyme "Apple Pie ABC," which first appeared in print in a book titled *Tom Thumb's Playbook to Teach Children Their Letters as soon as they can speak, being a new and pleasant method to allure little ones in the first principles of learning* (1747). If you want to read this book, look no further than the Baldwin Library; its facsimile is a lovely representation of an alphabet primer chapbook.

See Tom Thumb ſtand
In his Father's hand,

TOM THUMB's
PLAY-BOOK,
To teach CHILDREN their LETTERS as ſoon as they can ſpeak.

Being a new and pleaſant method to allure Little ONES in the firſt principles of Learning.

WORCESTER, (MASSACHUSETTS)
Printed by ISAIAH THOMAS,
And SOLD at his BOOK-STORE,
MDCCLXXXVI.

▶ ***Tom Thumb's Playbook to Teach Children Their Letters ...***, by Isaiah Thomas (1747).

Alphabet primers—also called "abecedarian books" or "concept books"—are stories that teach children their ABCs, usually in the form of rhymes or short stories that are motivated by the alphabet. In the case of "Apple Pie ABC," A is the eponymous apple pie, and the letters B-Z are verbs that describe what children do to the pie: "B bit it," "F fought for it," and so forth. In the earliest known print version of the story, X is lumped with "Y Z &," and the rhyme reads "Amperse and All Wished for a Piece in Hand."

It wasn't until the publication of *The History of the Apple Pie, an Alphabet for Little Masters and Misses* (1808, written by "Z"), that X began to get an illustration and verse. In this version, "Xerxes drew his sword for it," presumably to cut off a chunk of pie for himself.

The rhyme was so well known that several authors referred to the text in their own stories: Edward Lear parodied the lines in his poem "A was

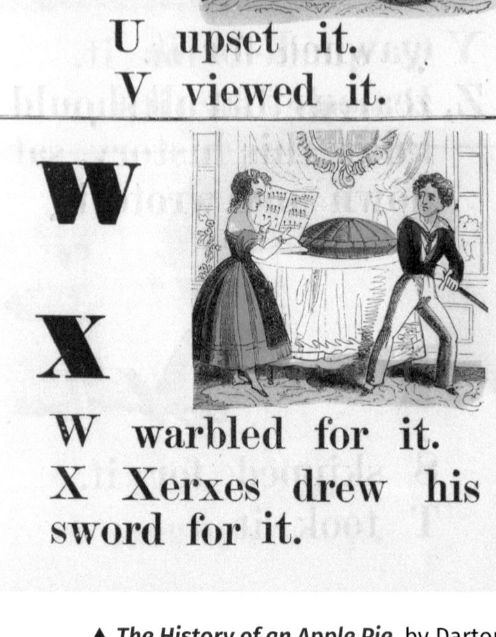

▲ ***The History of an Apple Pie,*** by Darton & Co. (1845).

▶ ***Apple-Pie ABC, Kriss Kringle Series,*** by McLoughlin Bros., Inc. (c.1897).

Once an Apple Pie," where Xerxes becomes the king from the Biblical Book of Esther. Our friend Xerxes was even mentioned by name in Dickens' essay "A Christmas Tree" (1850), and the "Apple Pie" rhyme makes an appearance in *Bleak House* (1853) as Dickens lambasts the British legal system.

While the Apple Pie alphabet primer did cross the pond in the eighteenth century, in America the most popular primer, was of course, *The New England Primer*. In this text, the ABCs are all Puritanical in nature, and X is again for King Xerxes ("Who did die/and so must you and I").

Modern readers may recognize Xerxes not from "Apple Pie" but instead from Edward Gorey's delightfully ghoulish picture book *The Gashelycrumb Tinies* (1963). In this gothic twist on the gentle abecedarian genre, Gorey pushes the boundaries of what abecedarian books are, and who they are for. Here, all the Tinies die tragic deaths brought about by accident or parental inattention, and X is no exception: "X is for Xerxes, devoured by mice," and the illustration brings to mind some shadowy scene from an Edgar Allan Poe story.

Whether as a king, a swordsman, or a child about to die in a Poe-etic fashion, Xerxes has hovered in the final pages of abecedarian stories for centuries. You can find him in the Baldwin between the covers of such works as *The Picture ABC Book with Stories* (1850), *Nursery ABC and Simple Speller* (1870), and *Little Boys and Girls ABC* (1884).

LESSON 24.
Is it a pin I see on the mat?
Yes, it is.
Get my hat for me,
I can go to see the nag.

XERXES.

YACHT.

LESSON 25.
The bee can fly: the cat can run and the cat can mew: the bee can fly, but can not run as the cat can.

LESSON 26.
The dog eat up the hen.
The cat eat up the rat.
The boy eat up the egg.

ZANY.

▲◀ **Nursery ABC and Simple Speller,** engraved by Edward P. Cogger, published by McLoughlin Bros., Inc. (1870).

Ramona Caponegro

is for Youthful Offenders

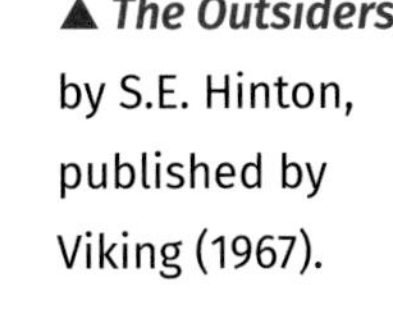

▲ ***The Outsiders,*** by S.E. Hinton, published by Viking (1967).

"Youthful offender" is an elastic term.

It has specific legal definitions, albeit definitions that vary across states and countries, but it also has generalized negative connotations that extend beyond legal terminology, as do the labels of "juvenile delinquent" and "criminal." Moreover, whether a person is considered a youthful offender in or out of a courtroom and for which offenses often depends on their race, gender, and socioeconomic status.

◀ ***United States Criminal Calendar,*** by Henry St. Clair, published by Charles Gaylord (1833).

"Come now, I've got my eye on you."
See Page 59

▲ ***Storm of Life,*** by Hesba Stretton, published by Religious Tract Society (1881).

▶ ***Monster,*** by Walter Dean Myers, illustrated by Christopher Myers, published by HarperCollins (1999).

British and American children's books have included legally sanctioned punishments for crimes and stigmatizing labels for offenders since at least the nineteenth century, when Great Britain was reconfiguring its prison system and the United States was creating one. Since then, children's books about youthful offenders have had a variety of aims, sometimes within the same story: serving as a cautionary tale, humanizing youthful offenders, maintaining the social and legal status quo, and challenging society and the legal system.

The temperance tract *It Won't Hurt You* (1868) cautions readers to avoid the first sip of alcohol, lest, like the character Frank Russel who cannot withstand temptation, they, too, wind up in prison or suffer worse fates. Though far less didactic, Walter Dean Myers's young adult novel *Monster* (1999) also suggests that Steve Harmon could have avoided incarceration if he had made different choices well before he was presented with the opportunity to participate in an armed robbery.

Yet while Myers encourages readers to question Steve's decisions, he never fails to show that Steve is a terrified, multidimensional teenager and not a monster, no matter what the prosecutor says. Similarly, in the young adult novel *The Outsiders* (1967), S.E. Hinton emphasizes the humanity of the Greasers, gang members who are usually dismissed or stereotyped because of their socioeconomic status and group affiliation. Likewise in the historical novel *The Witch of Blackbird Pond* (1958), Elizabeth George Speare reveals the all too human motivations of fear, anger, and loneliness that lead Kit Tyler to be accused of witchcraft.

Because the charges against Kit are dismissed, the legal system is also vindicated in the novel, with one vengeful woman depicted as the troublemaker, rather than a system in which unsubstantiated charges can too easily be filed against people perceived as outsiders. In *The Trial: More Links of the Daisy Chain* (1868), Charlotte Mary Yonge goes ever further to defend the integrity of the legal system, claiming that even though Leonard Ward is wrongfully convicted and clearly harmed by his imprisonment, the ordeal still benefits him because it strengthens his character.

Nevertheless, Yonge uses *The Trial* to criticize the separate system, a prison isolation practice. Thinking beyond one destructive practice, Mildred D. Taylor's historical novel, *Let the Circle Be Unbroken* (1981), highlights the racism inherent in the legal code of 1930s Alabama through the murder trial of T.J. Avery, a Black teenager, as well as Mrs. Lee Annie's blocked attempts at voter registration.

An increasing number of contemporary children's books feature youthful offenders and legal systems, and the Baldwin's holdings encourage us to ask what these contemporary books will tell future readers about our society's ideas of crime, justice, punishment, and rehabilitation.

▲ ***The Trial: More Links of the Daisy Chain,*** **by Mary Charlotte Yonge, published by Macmillan & Co. (1868).**

Z

Suzan Alteri

The zoetrope, an early animation device, paved the way for the modern motion picture.

is for Zoetrope

One of the most popular optical toys of the 19th century was the zoetrope, which produces the illusion of movement from a rapid succession of static images. Appropriately called "the wheel of life," (translated from the Greek) the device works by spinning a large metal drum with tiny vertical slits cut into its side. Viewers then spin the drum, look through the slits and as the static images spin, they appear animated. Think of a flipbook, only larger and more theatrical.

The zoetrope, an early animation device, paved the way for the modern motion picture. It was first invented in 1834 by British mathematician William Horner. The invention was based on Joseph Plateau's phenakisticope, a flat, cardboard disk attached to a handle, with slots cut out around the rim. When the user spun the disk and looked through the slots into a mirror, the reflected images appeared to be moving. Over thirty years later, William F. Lincoln, a Brown University student, patented the device that is known today.

The Baldwin's Zoetrope consists of a cylinder with an open top, placed on a central wooden base that allows the mechanism to spin when pushed. Placed on the bottom of the metal drum is a dark but colorful paper base (our version has three) of abstract geometrical shapes of expanding stars that only added to the hypnotic effect. Paper strips of still images depicted in a

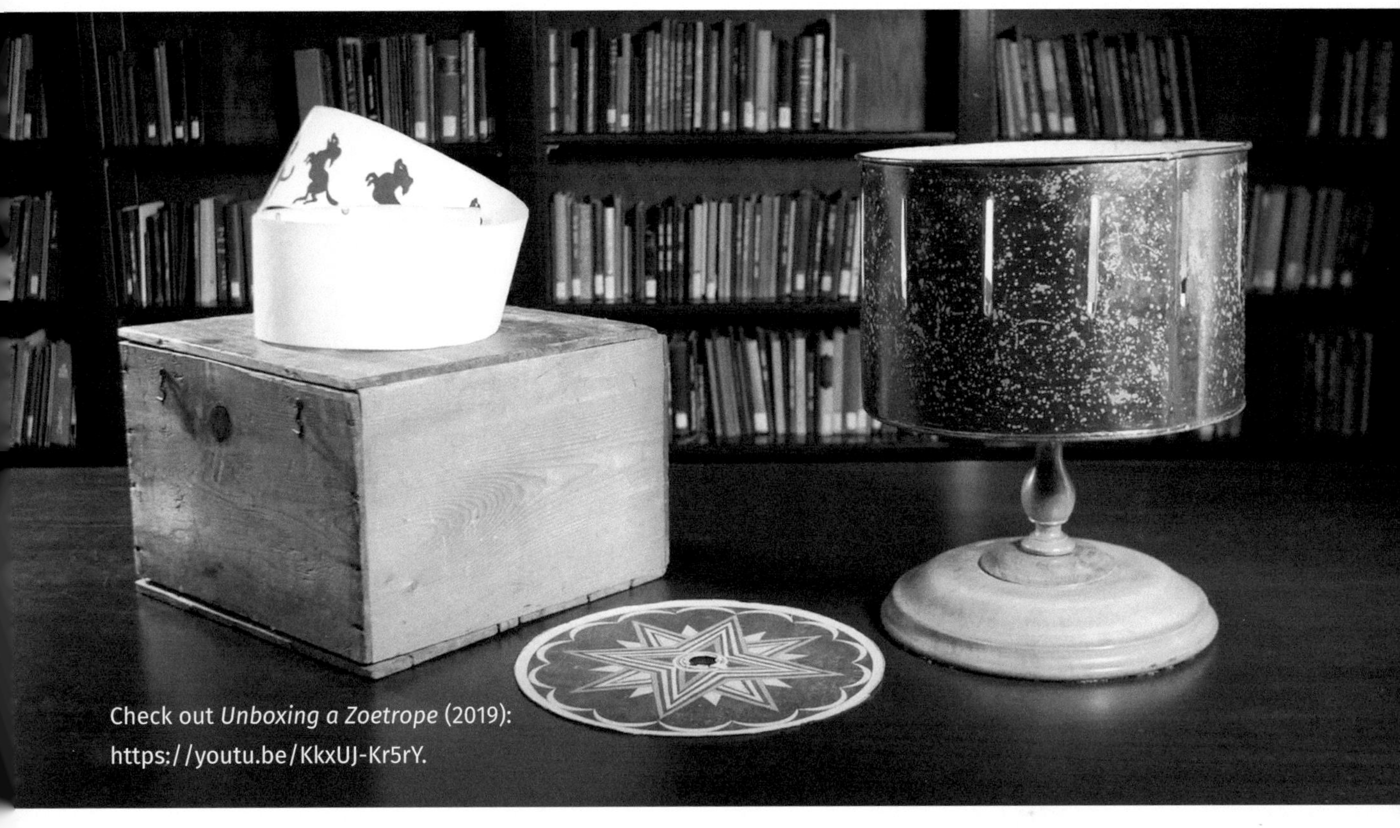
Check out *Unboxing a Zoetrope* (2019): https://youtu.be/KkxUJ-Kr5rY.

sequential pattern were placed along the sides of the drum. Once you spin the drum - viola – an instant crowd-pleaser. Both students, professors and visitors delight in watching this almost 100-year-old toy.

Marketed and sold by the London Stereoscopic and Photographic Company, the Zoetrope cost one guinea (one pound one shilling), which was more than most people could afford on such a luxury. But despite the high price, surviving sales numbers indicate the toy's popularity with middle class and wealthy customers. In the United States, Zoetropes were introduced by Milton Bradley now known for producing many of today's board games. A large zoetrope with life-size images was exhibited at the Grand International Exhibition of 1851.

With the zoetrope's rise to prominence, this Victorian era invention has secured a foothold in modern times and is found in displays across international cultures and borders. A 3D zoetrope featuring Pixar's *Toy Story* appeared in Disneyland as well as New York City's Museum of Modern Art in [year]. Additionally, the Ghibli Museum in Tokyo, Japan, features a 3D zoetrope of characters from the anime film *My Neighbor Totoro.*

Photo credit: Barbara Hood.

An Alphabet Tour of the Baldwin Library of Historical Children's Literature

Contributors

ALICE FOUND HERSELF FALLING DOWN WHAT SEEMED TO BE A VERY DEEP WELL

▶ ***Alice's Adventures in Wonderland***, by Lewis Carroll,illustrated by W. H. Walker, published by Dodd, Mead & Co. (1923).

Suzan Alteri

Librarian for the Arne Nixon Center for the Study of Children's Literature

California State University Fresno

Previously Curator of the Baldwin Library of Historical Children's Literature, her current research focuses on public review responses to Indigenous Picturebooks, multiethnic and diversity in children's literature, and archival pedagogy. She has published in *Education Libraries, Digital Defoe*, and the *Journal of Interactive Technology and Pedagogy*, and is the author of the digital bibliography "Guiding Science: Women Authored Science Books for Children 1790-1890."

EDITORIAL COLLECTIVE

H IS FOR HISTORICAL BIOGRAPHIES

U IS FOR UNUSUAL

Z IS FOR ZOETROPE

Poushali Bhadury

Assistant Professor of English

Middle Tennessee State University

Her research interests include comparative children's literature, postcolonial literature, South Asian book history, queer studies, and digital humanities. Her two current book projects include The Home and the World in (Post)Colonial Print Culture: Deb Sahitya Kutir and Bengali Children's Publishing (1940-1975), and a co-written monograph, Daddy Issues: Fathers in North American Girls' Literature.

EDITORIAL COLLECTIVE

Emily Brooks

Assistant Professor of Digital Culture and Design

Coastal Carolina University

She received her PhD in English and Graduate Certificate in Digital Humanities from the University of Florida in August 2020. She is a "makeademic" and loves to tinker with technology. Her research focuses on digitizing nontraditional books including touch-and-feel books, interactive and movable books, and treasure bindings. She uses emerging technologies like photogrammetry, 3D scanning, and more to create virtual replicas of movable books.

P IS FOR POP-UP

Ramona Caponegro

Curator of the Baldwin Library of Historical Children's Literature

University of Florida

A former children's literature professor at Eastern Michigan University, she has published essays about developing diverse children's literature courses, children's book awards, representations of incarceration in children's and young adult literature, and early readers. She co-wrote the documentary, *Tell Me Another Story: Diversity in Children's Literature*, and created educational materials for The Newbery Practitioner's Guide and the Ezra Jack Keats Foundation. She chaired the Pura Belpre Award and the Phoenix Picture Book Award Committees, co-chaired the Pura Belpre Award 25th Anniversary Task Force, and is a member of the 2023 Caldecott Committee.

S IS FOR SERIES

Y IS FOR YOUTHFUL OFFENDERS

Julie A. S. Cassidy

Assistant Professor of English

The City University of New York – Borough of Manhattan Community College (CUNY – BMCC).

Julie's articles include "Popular" in *Keywords for Children's Literature* and "Transporting Nostalgia: Little Golden Books as Souvenirs of Childhood" in the *Children's Literature Journal*. When she isn't wrangling professors as the Composition Coordinator or developing a new Children and Youth Studies Program, she likes reading young adult novels, making veggie tacos, and looking for horseshoe crab molts on Sandy Hook in New Jersey. Before moving to the Northeast, she spent many hours in the Baldwin Library of Historical Children's Literature as she completed her Ph.D. in English with a specialization in children's literature at the University of Florida.

G IS FOR GOLDEN BOOKS

John Cech

Professor of English

University of Florida

John Cech is an award-winning writer, teacher, scholar and critic who has been actively working in the field of children's literature for the past three decades. He was the recipient of the Anne Devereaux Jordan award and the Chandler Award of Merit for his contributions as a scholar and and as a public intellectual in the field of children's literature. He is also the author of books for children and works for adults, he has also been a frequent contributor of articles, essays, and reviews to such publications as *The New York Times Book Review, Washington Post Book World, The Christian Science Monitor, The Horn Book Magazine*, and *Children's Literature*. He currently serves as the Director of the University of Florida's Center for Children's Literature and Culture. Cech's recent research involves a documentary history of children's literature that makes use of the University of Florida's premier collection of children's books.

M IS FOR MOTHER GOOSE

Spencer Chalifour

PhD Candidate, English

University of Florida

His research focuses on comics and visual rhetoric. He was the lead organizer for the 14th Annual UF Comics and Graphic Novels Conference, "Comics Remixed: Adaptation and Graphic Narrative." He has also contributed to the interdisciplinary comics journal *ImageTexT* as an editor.

L IS FOR LITTLE BOOKS

Perry Collins

LibraryPress@UF Rights Consultant

George A. Smathers Libraries, University of Florida

Perry Collins is the Copyright and Open Educational Resources Librarian at the George A. Smathers Libraries at the University of Florida. She is the UF Lead on the dLOC as Data Project.

RIGHTS CONSULTANT

JoAnn Conrad

Folklorist and Cultural Historian

University of California Berkeley

Currently (Spring 2022) Conrad is the Fulbright Scholar in Folkloristic at the University of Iceland, where she teaches courses in Feminist theory and also lower division courses which use folklore to discuss issues of representation and power. Conrad has been working with issues of childhood and children's literature throughout her career to approach larger discursive fields and cultural phenomena. She was a research fellow at the Baldwin library, looking at children's book illustrators of the early 20th century, when the publication of children's literature was just in its early stages. She is particularly interested in women editors, like Louise Seaman Bechtel, and the personal and professional relationships they developed with authors and illustrators that were so fundamental to publishing in that era. Conrad's article is based on material that demonstrates this relationship between Bechtel and Berta and Elmer Hadder, the husband and wife illustrator/author team.

J IS FOR JUVENILE EDITORS

Jill Coste

Independent Scholar

University of Florida

Her research interests include contemporary YA literature, Golden Age children's literature, fairy tale retellings, and speculative fiction. Her work on the dystopian YA fairy tale has appeared in the edited collections *Race in Young Adult Speculative Fiction and Beyond the Blockbusters: Themes and Trends in Contemporary Young Adult Literature.*

T IS FOR TALKING BOOKS

Chelsea Dinsmore

Chair of Resource Description Services

George A. Smathers Libraries, University of Florida

Chelsea Dinsmore joined the University of Florida George A. Smathers Libraries in 2004. With a primary research focus on developing means to improve the accessibility of digital collections by rehabilitating legacy metadata, she also prioritizes converting legacy formats, like microfilm, to extend the research potential of and access to, historically significant content. Ms. Dinsmore holds an MLIS from the University of Texas at Austin and an MA in History from the University of Florida.

N IS FOR NEH

Richard Flynn

Professor Emeritus of English

Georgia Southern University

Richard Flynn is Professor Emeritus of English at Georgia Southern University, where he taught children's literature and modern and contemporary poetry for 30 years. He is the author of *Randall Jarrell and the Lost World of Childhood*, a collection of poems *The Age of Reason*, and many articles about poets including Elizabeth Bishop, June Jordan, Gwendolyn Brooks, Muriel Rukeyser, Jacqueline Woodson, and Marilyn Nelson.

V IS FOR VERSE

Kristen Gregory

Lecturer

University of Arizona

Kristen Gregory earned her PhD from the University of Florida in 2018, and her dissertation focused on the representation of exceptional children in American Cold War literature. During her time there, she designed courses on the gifted child in American culture, the evil child in American literature, and, of course, death and childhood in the Baldwin Library. It was this last class that inspired this entry. The final project for this course was a student-led collaborative exhibit on childhood and death, which can be found at http://cradleandgrave.omeka.net. Kristen currently teaches writing at the University of Arizona, where she still sometimes brings in *The New England Primer* and *The Gashlycrumb Tinies*, albeit now with a focus on genre analysis.

D IS FOR DEATH

Terry Harpold

Professor of English

University of Florida

Teaches nineteenth- and early twentieth century science fiction, image-text studies, and environmental humanities.

R IS FOR ROBINSON CRUSOE

Hélène Huet

European Studies Librarian

George A. Smathers Libraries, University of Florida

She holds a Ph.D in French and Francophone studies from Penn State University. Her research interests include Decadent literature as well as nineteenth-century French literature and history more broadly, the history of the book and publishing, and digital humanities. Her two current Digital Humanities projects are "Mapping Decadence" and the "World War I Diary of Albert Huet." She is also the Chair of the Collection Development Working Group of the Collaborative Initiative for French Language Collections (CINFL) and Chair of the Florida Digital Humanities Consortium.

U IS FOR UNUSUAL

Cari Keebaugh

Professor of English

North Shore Community College

By night she is an avid thespian. She particularly enjoys fairy tales, both onstage (whether she's playing the witch or the princess) and in the classroom (where she teaches their origins and evolution).

X IS FOR XERXES

Kenneth Kidd

Professor of English

University of Florida

He is the author of three books on topics related to children's literature and culture and the co-editor of four more. With Beth Marshall he co-edits the Routledge Children's Literature and Culture book series.

EDITORIAL COLLECTIVE
INTRODUCTION

O IS FOR *OUR YOUNG FOLKS*
Q IS FOR QUEER

Tracy MacKay-Ratliff

LibraryPress@UF Designer & Coordinator

George A. Smathers Libraries, University of Florida

She supports academic faculty collaborating and outside partnerships with the Libraries, and manages design projects from conception to production. For over 25 years, she has honed her visual communication skills in digital/print publishing, logo/brand development, and advertising/promotional design. As the designer for LibraryPress@UF, she develops creative designs and publications, including *SOURCE*, UF Libraries Magazine.

EDITORIAL COLLECTIVE
CREATIVE DIRECTION

Anuja Madan

Associate Professor of English

Kansas State University

She teaches courses on postcolonial literature, children's and young adult literature, and comics. Her primary research is on Indian children's literature and comics, with a focus on adaptations of Hindu mythological narratives. Her other areas of interest include postcolonial and multiethnic children's literature. A few of her articles have appeared in the anthologies The Routledge Companion to International Children's Literature, Graphic Novels for Children and Young Adults: A Collection of Critical Essays as well as the South Asian Review special issue on South Asian Graphic Narratives.

A IS FOR ANGLOPHONE

▲ ***The 3 Little Kittenss***, Pleasewell Series, published by McLoughlin Bros., Inc. (1890)

Noah Mullens

MA Candidate, English

University of Florida

He received his bachelor's degree in English and Philosophy in Fall 2019. His main areas of focus are children's literature, queer studies, and archival research. In recent years, he interned at the Baldwin Library and is now curating the digital exhibit "Historical Diversity and Representation in the Baldwin Library of Historical Children's Literature."

K IS FOR KITSCH

Megan A. Norcia

Project Manager, Roots of Compassion and Kindness Program

Florida Gulf Coast University

Meg taught in the SUNY system for sixteen years, creating undergraduate and graduate courses in children's and young adult literatures, British literature, and Career Prep for English Majors, publishing two scholarly monographs (*X Marks the Spot: Women Writers Map the Empire for British Children, 1790-1895*, Ohio UP; *Gaming Empire in Children's British Board Games, 1836-1860*, Routledge), and winning a Chancellor's Award for Excellence in College Teaching. She now works in the FGCU Integrated Studies Department where she teaches classes and manages the Roots of Compassion and Kindness Center, attempting to transform Southwest FL into a "kindness zone," in collaboration with campus and community groups, and elementary school partners.

I IS FOR IMPERIALISM

Katherine Nguyen

LibraryPress@UF Student Assistant

University of Florida

Katherine recently graduated from the University of Florida in Spring 2022 with a bachelor's degree in English. She is currently the student assistant with LibraryPress@UF acting as administrative, editorial, and open education support.

COPY EDITOR

Mary Roca

Ph.D. Student in the Department of English

University of Florida

Mary Roca earned her PhD at the University of Florida, where she studied U.S. children's literature. Her scholarly interests include girls' books, archival work, popular culture, and representations of schooling. She teaches literature, composition, and public speaking at Choate Rosemary Hall.

W IS FOR WOMAN

Rita Smith

Emeritus Curator

University of Florida

Rita Smith is a former Curator of the Baldwin Library of Historical Children's Literature. She collaborated on three major grants from the National Endowment for the Humanities to catalog, microfilm, and digitize materials from the Baldwin Library, along with building the collections. She brought the collections into the light for access.

B IS FOR BALDWIN

Laurie Taylor

Senior Director for Library Technology & Digital Strategies

George A. Smathers Libraries, University of Florida

She provides leadership for technology and partnerships with the University of Florida Libraries across the university, regionally, nationally, and internationally. She works closely with colleagues to sustain collaborations for building collections, community, and capacity, including for the Digital Library of the Caribbean (dLOC) and LibraryPress@UF. Her work is geared towards enabling a culture of radical collaboration that values and supports diversity, equity, and inclusion.

EDITORIAL COLLECTIVE

N IS FOR NEH

Robert Thomson

Associate Professor Emeritus of English

University of Florida

Left Queens' College, Cambridge in 1974 after receiving his Ph.D. and joined the faculty in English at the University of Florida where he taught (for the most part happily) until his retirement (entirely happily) in 2013. His teaching interests were in early-modern English literature, particularly Shakespeare, as well as Maori literature of New Zealand, British and American folklore, and studies in balladry and folksong with particular interest in the symbiotic relationship between oral and printed broadside and chapbook texts. He has published widely across his range of interests but now devotes much of his time to collecting and restoring antique and vintage writing instruments and collecting nineteenth-century postage stamps. He was one of the delegation members who visited Ruth Baldwin in Louisiana.

C IS FOR CHAPBOOK

Mariko Turk

Writing Center Consultant

University of Colorado Boulder

Mariko Turk graduated from the University of Pittsburgh with a BA in creative writing. She received her PhD in English from the University of Florida, with a concentration in children's literature. Currently, she works as a Writing Center consultant at the University of Colorado Boulder. In 2021, she published her debut Young Adult novel *The Other Side of Perfect* to critical acclaim.

F IS FOR FLORIDA

Anastasia Ulanowicz

Associate Professor of English

University of Florida

She received her Ph.D. in Cultural and Critical Studies from the University of Pittsburgh in 2006. Her research is primarily focused on the representation of intergenerational relationships and memory in children's literature and graphic narratives. Her first book, *Second-Generation Memory and Contemporary Children's Literature: Ghost Images* received the Children's Literature Association Book Award in 2015. She is also the co-editor (with Manisha Basu) of *The Aesthetics and Politics of Global Hunger* (Palgrave, 2018). She is currently collaborating with Marek Oziewicz on a book on the emerging genre of "Bloodlands fiction" in global children's literature, and she is also developing a book project on representations of post-1989 Eastern Europe in comics and graphic narratives. In 2021, she was a Fulbright Scholar at the University of Wroclaw, Poland.

E IS FOR EDUCATION

Bibliography

Abbott, Jacob. *Cousin Lucy Among the Mountains.* Clark, Austin & Co., 1852

____. *Learning to Talk; Or, Entertaining and Instructive Lessons in the Use of Language.* Harper & Brothers, 1855.

____. *Rollo Learning to Talk.* Weeks, Jordan & Company, 1839.

____. *Rollo Learning to Talk.* Sheldon & Company, 1865.

Adams, Robert C. *History of the United States in Rhyme.* Lothrop Publishing Co., c. 1884.

Adams, William and Matteson, Tompkins Harrison (ill.). *Cherry Stones – Or, the Charlton School: A Tale for Youth.* General Protestant Episcopal Sunday School Union, 1851.

Adams, William Taylor. *Four Young Explorers, or, Sight-Seeing in the Tropics.* Lee and Shepard, 1896.

Adventures of Peter Jones. Williams, Orton & Co., ND.

Alcott, Louisa May. *Little Women, or, Meg, Jo, Beth and Amy.* Roberts Brothers, 1868.

Alden, W. L. and Small, F. O. (ill.). *Loss of the Swansea.* D. Lothrop & Company, c. 1889.

Aldrich, Bertha and Snyder, Ethel. *Florida Sea Shells.* Houghton Mifflin, 1978.

Alger, Edith Goodyear. "Finger Play & Monday." *St. Nicholas Magazine*, Vol. 22 Part II, pg. 1046

Ames, Mary. *An A B C for Baby Patriots.* Dean and Son, 1899.

Babes in the Woods. William Dickes (printer) and Sampson, Low, Son & Co., 1861.

Bailey, Bernadine and Wiese, Kurt (ill.). *Picture Book of Florida.* A Whitman, 1949.

Baker, Ray Stannard. *The Boy's Book of Inventions.* Doubleday & McClure Co., 1899.

Ballantyne, R. M. *The Coral Island.* Collins. ND

Barrie, J. M. *Peter and Wendy.* Grosset & Dunlap, 1911.

Bates, Clara Doty. *On the Way to Wonderland.* D. Lothrop
& Co., c. 1885.

Baum, Frank L. and McCracken, James (ill.). *Aunt Jane's Nieces Out West.* Reilly & Britton Co., 1914.

Baum, Frank L. and Denslow, W. W. (ill.). *Father Goose:
His Book.* George M. Hill Company, c. 1899.

Beard, Gaffer Black. *A New History of Blue Beard.* John Adams, 1804.

Bechtel, Louise Seaman. Baldwin Library: Archive and Manuscript Collection. https://baldwin.uflib.ufl.edu/resources/archives-manuscripts-louise-seaman-bechtel/.

Bond, Michael and Lokvig, Tor. *Paddington Learns a Lesson.* Price, Stern, Sloan Inc. and Intervisual Communications, 1981.

Bolton, Sarah K. *Lives of Girls Who Became Famous.* Thomas Y. Cromwell, c. 1886.

Book About Animals. Rufus Merrill, 1850.

Boscawen, Mary Frances. *Conversations on Geography, or, The Child's First Introduction to Where He Is, and What Else There Is Besides.* Longman, Brown, Green, and Longmans, 1854.

Bradford, Sarah H. *Harriet Tubman, the Moses of Her People.* Cornith Books, 1961.

Brand, Theodor. *The Speaking Picture Book: A Special Book with Picture, Rhyme and Sound for Little People*, c. 1893.

Burnett, Frances Hodgson. *The Secret Garden*. Frederick A. Stokes Company, 1911.

Burroughs, Edgar Rice. *The Return of Tarzan*. Whitman Publishing Company, 1936.

Cabinet of Lilliput Stored with Instruction and Delight. J. Harris, 1802.

Campe, Joachim and Bewick, John (engraver). *The New Robinson Crusoe: An Instructive and Entertaining History, for the Use of Children of Both Sexes*. John Stockdale, 1789.

Canton, William and Robinson, Thomas Hastings (ill.). *Child's Book of Saints*. J. M. Dent & Co., 1898.

Carroll, Lewis C. and Tenniel, John (ill.). *Alice's Adventures in Wonderland*. Henry Altemus Company, c. 1897

____. and McManus, Blanche (ill.). *Alice's Adventures in Wonderland*. M. F. Mansfield and A. Wessels, c. 1899.

____. and Walker, W. H. (ill.). *Alice's Adventures in Wonderland*. Dodd, Mead & Co., 1923.

____. and Attwell, Mabel Lucie (ill.). *Alice in Wonderland*. Raphael Tuck & Sons, c. 1910.

____. and Tenniel, John (ill.). *Through the Looking-Glass and What Alice Found There*. Gilbert H. McKibbin, 1829.

Carter, David. *600 Black Spots: A Pop-Up Book for All Ages*. Little Simon, 2007.

Child, Lydia Maria (ed.). *Juvenile Miscellany*. John Putnam. 1826-1836.

Champney, Elizabeth and Champney, James Wells (ill.). *Three Vassar Girls in Italy*. Estes & Lauriat, 1885.

Cogger, Edward. *Nursery A B C and Simple Speller*. McLoughlin Bros., c. 1870.

Collodi, Carlo and Richardson, Frederick (ill.). *Pinocchio*. John C. Winston Company, c. 1923.

Cox, Palmer. *Queer People with Wings and Stings and Their Kweer Kapers*. Edgewood Publishing Company, c. 1895.

____. *Queer People Such as Goblins, Giants, Merry Men, and Monarchs*. Edgewood Publishing Company, 1888.

Crane, Walter. *The Baby's Opera: A Book of Old Rhymes with New Dresses*. McLoughlin Bros., 1878.

Crewdson, T. D. and Anelay, Henry (ill.). *Aunt Jane's Verses for Children*. Charles Gilpin, 1851.

Cupples, Mrs. George. *Our Parlour Panarama*. Thomas Nelson & Sons, 1882

Cupples, Mrs. George. *Shadows on the Screen, or, An Evening with the Children*. Thomas Nelson & Sons, 1883.

Darton, John Maw and Weir, Harrison (ill.). *Brave Boys Who Have Become Illustrious Men of Our Time: Forming Bright Examples For Emulation By the Youth of Great Britain*. Swan, Sonnenschein & Co., 1884.

Defoe, Daniel. *Adventures of Robinson Crusoe*. S. W. Partridge & Co., 1873.

____. *Adventures of Robinson Crusoe*. J. Harris and Son, 1821.

____, Grandville, J. J. and Proctor, John. *Adventures of Robinson Crusoe*. Henry Lea, 1880.

____. *Bysh's Edition of the Life of Robinson Crusoe, of York, Mariner: Who Lived Eight-and-Twenty Years in an Uninhabited Island*. John Bysh, 183-.

____, and Stothard, Thomas. *The Life and Adventures of Robinson Crusoe*. Ballantyne, 1881.

____, and Watson, John Dawson. *The Life and Adventures of Robinson Crusoe*. George Routledge & Sons, 1891.

____. *The Life and Most Surprizing Adventures of Robinson Crusoe, of York, Mariner: Who Lived Eight and Twenty Years in an Uninhabited*

Island on the Coast of America, Lying Near the Mouth of the Great River of Oroonoque: Having Been Cast on Shore by Shipwreck, Wherein All the Men Were Drowned but Himself: As Also a Relation How He was Wonderfully Deliver'd by Pyrates. Printed for A. Bettesworth at the Red-Lyon in Pater-Noster Row, F. Brotherton at the Bible, W. Meadows at the Angel in Corn-Hill, and E. Midwinter at the Looking-Glass on London-Bridge, 1724.

____, Finnemore, Joseph, Thompson, G. H., and Webb, Archibald. *The Life and Strange Surprising Adventures of Robinson Crusoe, of York, Mariner: As Related by Himself*. Ernest Nister and E. P. Dutton, 1985.

____, and Louis Rhead and Frederick Alfred Rhead (ills.). *The Life and Strange Surprising Adventures of Robinson Crusoe, of York, Mariner*. R. H. Russell, 1900.

____, and Pogany, Willy (ill.). *Robinson Crusoe*. George G. Harrap & Co., 1914.

____. *Robinson Crusoe Picture Book*. George Routledge and Sons, 187-.

____. *Robinson Crusoe in Pitman's Shorthand (Corresponding Style)*. Sir Isaac Pitman & Sons, Ltd., 1887.

Dean's New Book of Dissolving Pictures. Dean and Son, 1862.

Denslow, W. W. *Denslow's A B C*. G W Dillingham Co., 1903.

Denslow, W. W. *Denslow's Mother Goose A. B. C. Book*. G. W. Dillingham Co., 1904.

Dodge, Mary Mapes (ed.). *St. Nicholas Magazine*. Scribner. 1873-1943.

____. *When Life is Young: A Collection of Verses for Boys and Girls*. The Century Co., 1894.

Douglas, Marjorie Stoneman. *Alligator Crossing: A Novel*. John Day Company, 1959.

Duff, Alexander. *Charlotte, the Hindoo Orphan: and Other Tales from the East*. Unwin Brothers, 1877.

Eaton, Frances and Bridgman, Lewis J. *The Queer Little Princess and Her Friends*. D. Lothrop Company, c. 1888.

Edgar, John George. *Boy Princes: The Story of Their Lives*. Darton & Hodge, 1864.

Eggleston, Edward. *Queer Stories for Boys and Girls*. Charles Scribner's Sons, 1884.

Emerson, Alice B. *Ruth Fielding in the Great Northwest*. Cupples & Leon, 1921.

Epstein, Sam and Beryl and Frame, Paul (ill.). *Harriet Tubman: Guide to Freedom*. Garrard Publishing Company, 1968.

Farjean, Eleanor and Herbert. *Heroes and Heroines*. E. P. Dutton & Co., Inc., c. 1940.

Ferris, Helen Josephine, Moore, Virginia, and Moncure, Harriet (ill.). *Girls Who Did: Stories of Real Girls and Their Careers*. E. P. Dutton & Co., c. 1927.

Fillmore, Parker. *Little Question in Ladies' Rights*. John Lane Co., c. 1927.

Fowler, Daniel. *Delightful Stories of Travel at Home and Abroad*. World Bible House, 1895.

Foxe, John. *Foxe's Book of Martyrs*. Frederick Warne and Co., 1887.

Fun at the Circus. Raphael Tuck & Sons, 1892.

Geography in Easy Dialogues. Whittingham and Rowland, 1816.

Giraud, S. Louis. *A B C in Living Models: A Book in which All the Letters of the Alphabet Stand Up in Life-Like Form When the Pages Open*. Strand Publications, c. 1935.

____. *Bookano Zoo Animals in Fact, Fancy and Fun*. Strand Publications, 1935.

Goldsmith, Oliver and Caldecott, Randolph. *An Elegy on the Death of a Mad Dog*. George Routledge and Sons., 1885-1892.

Gorey, Edward. *The Dwindling Party*. Random House, 1982.

Gorey, Edward. *The Gashlycrumb Tinies, or, After the Outing*. Dodd, Mead & Company and Simon and Schuster, Inc., 1981.

Gould, Chester. *The Adventures of Dick Tracy Detective*. Whitman Publishing Company, 1932.

Goulding, F. R. and Weir, Harrison (ill.). *Robert and Harold, or, The Young Marooners*. G. Routledge. & Co., 1856

Hale, Sarah Josepha. *Lessons from Women's Lives*. McFarlane and Erskine, 1877.

Hield, Mary. *Living Pages from Many Ages*. Cassell, Petter, Galpin & Co., 1879.

Hinton, S. E. *The Outsiders*, Viking Press, 1967.

History of Cinderella and Her Glass Slipper. Orlando Hodgson, c. 1835.

History of Little Fanny: Exemplified in a Series of Figures. S. and J. Fuller, 1810.

Hope, Laura Lee. *Outdoor Girls in Florida*. Grosset & Dunlap, c. 1913.

Hughes, Thomas. *Tom Brown's School Days*. Ward, Lock & Co., 18--.

It Won't Hurt You. American Baptist Publication Society, c. 1868.

Jackson, J. J. *Nonsense for Girls*. McLouglin Bros., c. 1880.

Janeway, James. *A Token for Children, Being an Exact Account of the Conversion, Holy and Exemplary Lives and Joyful Deaths of Several Young Children*. Zachariah Fowle, 1771.

Jenness, Mary. *Twelve Negro Americans*. Friendship Press, 1936.

Keene, Carolyn. *The Secret of the Old Clock*. Grosset & Dunlap, 1930.

Kilner, Dorothy and Croome, W. (ill.). *The Life and Perambulations of a Mouse*. George S. Appleton, 1846.

Kilner, Dorothy. *The Rational Brutes, or Talking Animals*. B. & J. Johnson, 1801.

Knatchbull-Hugessen, Edward H. *Queer Folk: Seven Stories*. Macmillan &. Co., 1874.

Knox, Thomas Wallace. *Adventures of Two Youths in a Journey to Africa*. Harper & Brothers, 1884.

____. *Adventures of Two Youths in a Journey to Ceylon and India*. Harper & Brothers, 1882.

____. *Boy Travellers on the Congo: Adventures of Two Youths in a Journey with Henry M. Stanley "Through the Dark Continent."* Sampson Low, Marston, Searle & Rivington, 1888.

Kronheim, Joseph Martin. *My First Picture Book*. George Routledge & Sons, c. 1871.

Kubasta, Vojtech. *Tip & Top and the Moon Rocket*. Bancroft & Co. Ltd., 1964.

Lawrence, Jacob and Kraus, Robert. *Harriet and the Promised Land*. Simon and Schuster, 1968.

Le Baron, Grace. *Queer Janet*. Lee and Shepard Publishers, 1897.

Lenski, Lois. *Strawberry Girl*. J. B. Lippincott Company, 1945.

Little Boys and Girls A B C. McLoughlin Brothers, 1884.

Little Verses for Good Children. J. Metcalf, 1840.

Longacre, James Barton. *Life of Christian F. Swartz: An Early Missionary in India*. American Sunday School Union, 1830.

Lowrey, Janet Sebring and Tenggren, Gustaf (ill.). *The Poky Little Puppy*. Simon & Schuster, Inc., 1942.

MacDonald, George and Hughes, Arthur. *At the Back of the North Wind*. George Routledge & Sons, 1872.

Marston, Anne Wright. *Children of India: Written for the Children of England*. Religious Tract Society, Pardon and Sons, 1884.

McDougall, Henriette. *Letters from Sarawak: Addressed to a Child*. Grant and Griffith, 1854.

Meade, L. T. *Four On an Island: A Story of Adventure*. W & R. Chambers, Ltd., 1899.

Meggendorfer, Lothar. *Always Jolly: A Movable Toybook*. H. Grevel & Co., 1891.

____. *Moving Picture Series*. International News Company, c. 1884.

____. *Princess Rose-Petal and Her Adventures*. H. Grevel and Frederick A. Stokes, 1899.

Miller, Olive Thorne. *Queer Pet's at Marcy's*. E. P. Dutton & Co., c. 1880.

Miloche, Hilda and Kane, Wilma. *The Paper Doll Wedding*. Simon & Schuster, Inc., 1951.

Montieth, James. *Introduction to the Manual of Geography*. A. S. Barnes and Company, 1871.

My Pet Box of Books. Leavitt & Allen, 185-.

Myers, Walter Dean and Myers, Christopher (ill.). *Monster*. HarperCollins, 1999.

Nast, Elsa Ruth and Malvern, Corinne (ill.). Fun with Decals. Simon & Schuster, Inc., 1952.

New England Primer, Improved. Sidney Babcock, 1826-1830.

Packer, Eleanor. *Charles Dickens' David Copperfield*. Whitman Publishing Company, 1934

Perrault, Charles. *Histories, or, Tales of Past Times*. Philip Rose, 1800.

Petry, Ann. *Harriet Tubman: Conductor on the Underground Railroad*. Thomas Y. Cromwell Company, 1955.

Pienkowski, Jan and Lokvig, Tor. *Haunted House*. Heinemann, S. A. Carvajal, and Intervisual Communications, 1979.

Pintard, J. Antoine. *Spectacle Asiatique Danse et Voltige sur la Corde avec sans Balancier*. Aubert, c. 1835.

Pity the Negro; or, An Address to Children, on the Subject of Slavery. Francis Westley, 1825.

Pleasing Toy. J. Metcalf, 1835.

Rackham, Arthur. *Mother Goose the Old Nursery Rhymes*. William Heinemann, 1913.

Rathborne, St. George. *Boy Cruisers, Or, Paddling in Florida*. A. L. Burt, c. 1893.

Religious Experience and Death of Eliza Van Wyck. American Tract Society, 1830-1832.

Robert and Jane. William T. Truman, ND.

Robin Hood's Garland: Being a Complete History of All the Notable Exploits Performed by Him and His Merry Men: to Which is Prefixed a Full Account of His Birth &c., James Kendrew, 180?

Sabuda, Robert, Reinhart, Matthew, and de Paola, Tomie. *Brava, Strega Nona: A Heartwarming Pop-Up Book*, G. P. Putnam's Sons, 2008.

Sabuda, Robert and Lewis, C. S. *The Chronicles of Narnia*. HarperCollins, 2007.

____. *The Wonderful Wizard of Oz*. Little Simon, 2000.

Sands, Benjamin and Poupard, J. (engraver). *Metamorphosis, or, A Transformation of Pictures: With Poetical Explanations: for the Amusement of Youth*. Solomon Wiatt, 1807.

Scarry, Richard. *Cars and Trucks*. Western Publishing Company, 1959

Scarry, Richard and Lokvig, Tor. *Richard Scarry's Mr. Frumble: Smallest Pop-Up Book Ever!* Western Publishing Company, 1992.

Schroeder, Alan and Pinkney, Jerry (ill.). *Minty: A Story of Young Harriet Tubman*. Dial Books for Young Readers, 1996.

Scripture Female Portraits, in Verse: For the Instruction of Youth. E. Wallis, 1820.

Scripture Picture Alphabet. Thomas Nelson & Sons, c. 1880.

Scudder, John. *Letters to Sabbath School Children on the Condition of the Heathen*. American Sunday School Union, 1843.

Shane, Ruth and Harold and Wilkin, Eloise Burns. *The New Baby*. Golden Press, 1948.

Shelton, W. H. *Pussy's Queer Babies, and Other Stories*. Estes and Lauriat, 1887.

Sherwood, Mary Martha. *Little Henry and His Bearer*. American Sunday School Union, 1845-1853.

Shimek, John Lyle and Scarry, Richard (ill.). *Cowboy Stamps*. Simon & Schuster, Inc., 1957.

Sleeping Beauty Pantomime Toy Book. McLouglin Bros., c. 1870.

Speare, Elizabeth George. *The Witch of Blackbird Pond*. Houghton Mifflin, 1958.

St. Clair, Henry. *United States Criminal Calendar, Or, An Awful Warning to the Youth of America; Being an Account of the Most Horrid Murders, Piraces, Highway Robberies, &c. &c.* Charles Gaylord, 1833.

Standing, Herbert. *The Children of Madagascar*. Religious Tract Society, 1887.

Stein, Mini and Wilkinream, Eloise (ill.). *We Help Daddy*. Western Publishing Co., 1962.

Stone, William. *My First Voyage: A Book for Youth*. Simpkin, Marshall & Co., 1860.

Stowe, Harriet Beecher and Morse, George Hazen (ill.). *Queer Little People*. Ticknor and Fields, 1867.

Stretton, Hesba. *The Storm of Life*. Religious Tract Society, 1881.

Striker, Fran and Weisman, Robert R. (ill.). *The Green Hornet Strikes!* Whitman Publishing Company, 1940.

Sutton, Amos. *The Hindoo Foundling Girl, Or, The History of Little Polly S*****:* Related By a Mother to Her Children; A True Tale. Baptist Mission Press, 1834.

Swift, Hildegarde Hoyt and Daugherty, James (ill.). *The Railroad to Freedom: A Story of the Civil War*. Harcourt Brace & Company, 1932.

Tales of Shakespeare in Verse. Frederick Warne & Co., c. 1880.

Talking Animal Book, 195-.

Taylor, Isaac. *Biography of a Brown Loaf: with Five Engravings on Wood and a Frontispiece*. John Harris, 1829.

Taylor, Mildred D. *Let the Circle Be Unbroken*. Dial Press, 1981.

Temperance Alphabet for Bands of Hope. William Tweedie, 1871.

The Children in the Wood Restored, by Honestas, the Hermit of the Forest, or, Perfidy Detected. J. G. Rusher, 182?

The History of Apple Pie. Darton & Co., c. 1845.

The Prodigal Daughter: Being a Strange Wonder Relation of a Young Lady in Bristol, Who, Because Her Parents Would Not Support Her in Her Extravagance, Bargained with the Devil to Poison Them; How an Angel Informed Her Parents of Her Design; How She Lay in a Trance Four Days; How She Came to Life Again, &c. &c. Zachariah Fowles, 1767?

The Six Good Dogs Who Always Did as They Were Bid. T. Nelson & Sons, 1874.

The 3 Little Kittens. McLoughlin Bros., 1890.

Thomas, Isaiah. *New A B C*. I. Thomas, Jun., 1805.

____. *Tom Thumb's Playbook to Teach Children Their Letters as Soon as They Can Speak*. Isaiah Thomas, 1786.

Trowbridge, John Townsend, Hamilton, Gail, and Larcom, Lucy (eds.). *Our Young Folks: An Illustrated Magazine for Boys and Girls*. Ticknor and Fields, 1865-1873.

Tucker, Charlotte Maria (A. L. O. E.). *Edith & Her Ayah and Other Stories*. T. Nelson and Sons, 1873.

Twenty Four Pictures from Mother Goose: With Full Directions for Coloring. S. W. Tilton and Co., c. 1881.

Vandegrift, Margaret. *Dead Doll and Other Verses.* Ticknor & Co., 1889.

Venning, Mary Anne. *A Geographical Present; Being Descriptions of The Principal Countries of the World.* Darton, Harvey and Darton, 1818.

Wakefield, Priscilla. *A Family Tour through the British Empire.* Jacob Johnson & Co., 1804.

____. *The Traveller in Africa: Containing Some Account of the Antiquities, Natural Curiosities, and Inhabitants of Such Parts of that Continent and its Islands, as Have Been Explored by Many Europeans; the Route Traced on a Map for the Entertainment and Instruction of Young Persons.* Darton, Harvey, and Darton, 1814.

____. *The Traveller in Asia, or, A Visit to the Most Celebrated Parts of the East Indies and China: With an Account of the Manners of the Inhabitants, Natural Productions, and Curiosities: For the Instruction and Entertainment of Young Persons.* Darton, Harvey, and Darton, 1817.

Walt Disney Studios. *The "Pop-up" Minnie Mouse.* Blue Ribbon Books, 1933.

Weatherford, Carole Boston and Nelson, Kadir (ill.). *Moses: When Harriet Tubman Led Her People to Freedom.* Hyperion Books for Children, 2006.

Weedon, L. L. and Hardy, E. Stuart. *Fairy Tales in Wonderland.* Ernest Nistor and E. P. Dutton, c. 1910.

Wehr, Julian. *Animated Antics in Playland.* Saalfield Publishing Co., 1946.

____. *Exciting Adventures of Finnie the Fiddler.* Cupples & Leon Company, c. 1942.

Whittington and His Cat. Sidney's Press. Printed by John Babcock and Son & S. Babcock & Co., 1824.

Wild Animal Stories: A Panorama Picture Book. Ernest Nister, 1897.

Woodward, Alice (ill.). *Banbury Cross and Other Nursery Rhymes.* J. M. Dent & Co., 1895.

Woodworth, Francis C. *The A B C Picture Book: with Stories.* Clark, Austin & Co., 1850.

Wordsworth, William and King, Agnes Gardner (ill.). *We Are Seven.* Meissner & Buch, 1892.

Wyler, Rose and Gergely, Tibor (ill.). *Exploring Space.* Golden Press, 1958.

Ye Book of Sense: A Companion to the Book of Nonsense. Porter & Coates, 1878?

Yonge, Charlotte Mary and Frolich, Lorenz (ill.). *Little Lucy's Wonderful Globe.* D. Lothrop & Co. and G. T. Day & Co., 1872.

____. *The Trial: More Links of the Daisy Chain.* Macmillan & Co., 1868.

"The Cat vanished quite slowly, ending with the grin"

▲ ***Alice's Adventures in Wonderland,*** by Lewis Carroll, edited by Florence Milner, illustrated by Fanny Y. Cory, published by Rand McNally and Co. (c.1902).